CHINESE GORDON: A SUCCINCT RECORD OF HIS LIFE

Published @ 2017 Trieste Publishing Pty Ltd

ISBN 9780649547180

Chinese Gordon: A Succinct Record of His Life by Archibald Forbes

Edited by Trieste Publishing Pty Ltd.
Cover @ 2017

www.triestepublishing.com

ARCHIBALD FORBES

CHINESE GORDON: A SUCCINCT RECORD OF HIS LIFE

CHINESE GORDON

A SUCCINCT RECORD OF HIS LIFE

BY

ARCHIBALD FORBES

LONDON
GEORGE ROUTLEDGE AND SONS
BROADWAY, LUDGATE HILL
NEW YORK: 9, LAFAYETTE PLACE
1884

CONTENTS.

CHAPTER I.

PAGE

EARLY DAYS, AND THE CRIMEA 1

CHAPTER II.

CHINESE GORDON IN CHINA 23

CHAPTER III.

GRAVESEND AND THE EQUATOR 116

CHAPTER IV.

GOVERNOR-GENERAL OF THE SOUDAN 158

CHAPTER V.

INDIA, CHINA, AND THE CAPE 204

CHAPTER VI.

BRITISH PLENIPOTENTIARY IN THE SOUDAN 221

CHINESE GORDON.

A SUCCINCT RECORD OF HIS LIFE.

CHAPTER I.

EARLY DAYS, AND THE CRIMEA.

THE character of Charles George Gordon is unique. As it unfolds itself in its curiously varied, but never contradictory aspects, the student is reminded of the attributes of Sir Lancelot, of Bayard, of Cromwell, of John Nicholson, of Arthur Connolly, of Havelock, of Balfour of Burley, of Livingstone, of Hedley Vicars; but Gordon's individuality stands out in its incomparable blending of masterfulness and tenderness, of strength and sweetness. His high nature is made the more chivalrous by his fervent piety. His absolute trust in God guides him serenely through the sternest difficulties. Because of that he is alone in no solitude, he is depressed in no extremity. The noble character has its complement in a

B

keen sense of humour. No matter how sombre the situation, if there be a comic side to any incident, Gordon sees it and enjoys it. That he has lived through strain so intense, and toil so arduous, is probably due to the never-failing fountain of blitheness that wells up in his nature. He must be richly endowed with the rare gift of personal magnetism. Without that men have attained to greatness : but never with the scantiness of means at command, that has thrown Gordon back mainly on the resources of his own personality ; nor ever with the scrupulousness that has been one of the most strongly marked traits of his career. This may be a plodding and prosaic age ; but no age can be so conventionalised that a man of Gordon's attributes may not find his opportunities to perform achievements the lustre of which stirs the astonishment and admiration of peoples who can yet appreciate the gifts that alone render those achievements possible. Gordon's modesty is great, but it would be unnatural and impossible that he should not feel an honest pride in the implicit confidence that leans on his ability to perform, single-handed, the seemingly impossible. This unique unanimity of confidence has been earned by deeds, not words; no arts have fostered its growth; it may be said to have come almost in spite of the man in whom it is reposed.

Gordon comes of a race of soldiers. His great-grandfather belonged to "Johnny Cope's" hapless command, as an officer in Lascelles' Regiment (now the 1st Battalion Lancashire Regiment), and was taken prisoner at Prestonpans by Prince Charlie's "highland host," to find a kinsman, Sir William Gordon, of Park, fighting under the Stuart banner. He was paroled through the interposition of the Duke of Cumberland, who was his patron, and the godfather of the son of his who was the grandfather of " Chinese Gordon." That son naturally entered the army, and saw varied and plentiful service. He fought at Minorca, at the siege of Louisburg, in what was then French Canada, and on the Plains of Abraham with the gallant Wolfe. In 1773 he married a Miss Clarke, the sister of a Northumbrian clergyman. By her he had four sons, the third of whom, Henry William, born in 1786, was the father of Charles George Gordon, the subject of this memoir.

Henry William Gordon was a gunner, a fine soldier, a man of the most scrupulous honour, of a temperament better suited, perhaps, for command than for obedience, but a man of remarkable geniality, and possessed of an inexhaustible fund of humour. He lived to be proud of his son, yet it has been told that so high was his ideal of the character of the British officer, that he had no pleasure in learning that his son had accepted the command of an alien and barbarian force, notwithstanding the honour of his selection therefor, and the brilliancy of his achievements in that position. He attained the rank of Lieutenant-General in the service in which he may be said to have been born, and in which he spent a long life. He was well mated in his wife, who had been a Miss Enderby, the daughter of a man of somewhat remarkable character. A London merchant and shipowner, some vessels of his mercantile fleet are historical. Those were two of Samuel Enderby's ships, chartered by the East India Company, and laden with cargoes of tea, that lay at their moorings in Boston Harbour on that evening of 1773, when Charles Adams stood up in the Old South Church and uttered

the words, " This meeting can do nothing more
to save the country !" That same night the sham
Indians boarded Enderby's ships, hauled on deck
the chests of the tea that formed their cargo,
broke them up and threw their contents over-
board, while the approving citizens crowding the
wharf listened in grim silence. When Phillip
gave the signal to " the first fleet " to cast anchor
in Sydney Cove, of the six transports that had
carried the convicts to found the new settlement,
some were ships chartered by the Government
from Charles Gordon's maternal grandfather.
His whalers opened up the fisheries in the Ant-
arctic Ocean, among the Islands of the South
Pacific, and in Japanese Waters, and made important geographical discoveries while they
were cruising with intent to " fill up " with oil.

Gordon's mother, Mr. Hake, in his " Story of
Chinese Gordon," describes as " a remarkable
woman. She possessed a perfect temper ; she
was always cheerful under the most trying
circumstances, and she was always thoughtful of
others ; she contended with difficulty without
the slightest display of effort ; and she had a
genius for making the best of everything.
During the Crimean War her anxieties were

interminable; she had three sons and several near kinsmen at the front. She was perfectly equal to the strain. Her hopefulness remained unclouded; all day long did she busy herself with the wants of others at home and in the field; while a duty remained to be done, or a kindness to be bestowed, her sunny energy maintained her at her work." This admirable woman—worthy mother of a noble son—gave her husband eleven children, five sons and six daughters. Of the sons three entered the army, and two are living. Of these two the younger is Charles George Gordon, he who now at the age of fifty-one—he was born at Woolwich, January 28th, 1833—is engaged in the work of the pacification of the Soudan.

Of Gordon's boyhood there is little to relate. A soldier's son, he shared some at least of the paternal migrations on military duty, for we hear of his having been in the Ionian Islands when his father was in command of the artillery there. He was prepared at Taunton for the Royal Military Academy, which he entered when as yet he had not completed his fifteenth year. His health in youth gave no promise of the phenomenal endurance which later in life he has undergone with surprising immunity from serious illness. " He was not strong," says Mr. Hake, "and this may account for his having done nothing really noteworthy either at school or at his later examinations. In this part of his story there was always humour, and now and then there were flashes of that resolution and energy which have since shown themselves in so many ways, and to such splendid purpose. Once, for instance, during his cadetship at the Academy, he was rebuked for incompetence, and told that he would never make an officer; whereupon he tore the epaulets from his shoulders and flung them at his superior's feet." As an instance of "resolution and energy" the anecdote proves rather too much. General Gordon has still a temper, and can "fly out" on occasion, but he is too good a soldier to justify the insubordination which it discloses, assuming the anecdote to be true. He must have worked hard at the Academy, and "incompetence" could hardly have been chargeable against a lad who came out so well as to win his appointment to the Royal Engineers. To that distinguished scientific corps he was gazetted as second lieutenant in July, 1852 ; so that he was nineteen and a-half years of age when he began his military career.

For two years he was at desk duty at Pembroke, preparing the plans for the fortifications that have since been constructed about the entrance to Milford Haven. The lad must have been eating his heart as he worked with rule and pencil, while more fortunate fellows were sailing eastward to where Sevastopol frowned over the waters of the Black Sea; but the time was coming when there should be other work than plan-making for a capable and resolute officer. He got the route for the Crimea in December, 1854, and on New Year's Day, 1855, the *Golden Fleece* carried him into that maritime chaos, the harbour of Balaclava. He landed in the very middle of the terrible " black winter." Everywhere prevailed misery, disease, and discontent. The great storm of the 14th November had gone far to ruin the encampments, and had shipwrecked a great fleet of vessels laden with stores that would have mitigated the rigour of the bitter winter. What of the cavalry horses Balaclava had left were dying at their picket ropes of cold and inanition. Fuel was not less cruelly scarce than

was food. On the squalor, hunger, and general
wretchedness cholera had supervened, and the
ranks were thinning faster than if every day had
furnished a hard fought skirmish. The French
were getting on with their trench work, but the
English had to concentrate their attention on
the too often unsuccessful effort to keep alive.
So in the lull of work the young engineer officer
seems to have been neglected if not forgotten,
and it was not until he had been landed a
month that he was detailed for his first turn of
service in the trenches. His duties thence-
forward until the fall of Sevastopol were simply
those of a junior officer of engineers, consisting
mainly in the superintendence of the execution
of the plans for the details of the siege operations devised by the superior officers of the
" scientific corps." This work entailed the most
arduous and continuous labour, all but chronic
exposure to hostile fire, not a little risk, when
out to the front either reconnoitring for the site
for a new parallel or a further advanced battery,
or when engaged in laying out the "trace" with
tape line and pegs, of being the recipient of an
accidental bullet from our own side ; the danger
also of being abandoned out in the front, because

of a sudden scare in the advanced lines behind ·
the adventurous pioneer, and of being either
shot down or made prisoner by a sudden sortie.
The earliest task set him, says Mr. Hake, was
to effect a junction by means of rifle pits between
the French and English sentries posted in
advance of the trenches; and in a letter home
he describes how "after being first fired upon
by the English sentries, and then by the Russian
pickets, and how often the working party and
sentries under his command had bolted, he was
able to carry out his first definite order on active
service."

The engineer service in the siege of Sevastopol never received the recognition which it
most justly merited, because of the devotion,
skill, and bravery of the officers who performed
it. Kinglake scarcely refers to it, and William
Howard Russell does not often allude to any engineer officer, except that most brilliant and ill-
fated officer whose career the late Col. Chesney
so vividly sketched in the paper entitled " Gordon of Gordon's Battery." The same gifted
author, in another paper, takes occasion to say
something of the character his Crimean service
earned for that gallant officer's junior of the

same name. Of the latter Chesney writes :
" Gordon had first seen war in the hard school
of the ' black winter ' of the Crimean War. In
his humble position as an engineer subaltern
he had attracted the notice of his superiors, not
merely by his energy and activity (for these are
not, it may be asserted, uncommon characteris-
tics of his class), but by an extraordinary aptitude for war, developing itself amid the trench-
work before Sevastopol in a personal knowledge
of the enemy's movements such as no other
officer attained. ' We used always to send him
out to find what new move the Russians were
making,' was the testimony given to his genius
by one of the most distinguished officers he
served under."

It was in the acquisition of this knowledge in
the course of sedulously constructing batteries
that Charles Gordon spent the spring of 1855,
on that bleak Crimean plateau. Russell thus
speaks of the spectacle the front presented in
March as the result of the labour expended on
works and counter-works :—" The front of Sevastopol, between English, French and Russians, looks like a large graveyard, covered as it
is with freshly-made mounds of dark earth in all

directions." In the performance of duties involving so much exposure, he must have had innumerable narrow escapes. One of these, when a bullet from one of the Russian rifle-pits passed within an inch of his head, he dismisses in a letter home with the terse comment: "They (the Russians) are very good marksmen ; their bullet is large and pointed." The engineer officers were severely taxed and exceptionally exposed during the preparations for the second bombardment in April, for the fourth parallel had to be constructed within six paces of the Russian rifle-pits, and during its continuance, when an embrasure was struck and injured by the return cannonade, it devolved upon them to set an example by freely exposing themselves when repairs were being made under fire. Gordon escaped untouched, amid the numerous casualties in the trenches, although constantly in the forefront of danger, and engaged in the resistance made to sortie after sortie from the Redan position of the Russians. In a letter home written during the bombardment he expresses himself with some confidence in regard to what Russell calls the " golden opportunity " for an assault not taken advantage of when the

mass of the Sevastopol garrison had been sent
out to reinforce Liprandi, in anticipation of his
being attacked, of which there was no intention
in the allied camp.   Gordon writes : " I think
we might have assaulted on Monday, but the
French do not seem to care about it.   The
garrison is 25,000, and on that day we heard
afterwards that only 8,000 were in the place,
as the rest had gone to repel an attack (fancied)
of ours at Inkermann."

From April 30, the advance of trench-work in
the English front was almost at a standstill until
the Mamelon, which enfiladed our advance works,
should fall ; but Gordon with his comrades was
unremittingly busy in preparing for the third
bombardment, which unprecedentedly stupendous artillery duel began on June 6.   Naturally
Gordon was in the trenches, and he was returned
among the wounded, but his injury was merely
a contusion from a stone which a round shot
had thrown up, and he did not allow it to dis-
able him from duty.   On the following day the
French carried the Mamelon, and were able to
hold it, but they were repulsed in their effort to
storm the Malakoff, and our attempt on the
Redan, which was led by Sir John Campbell,

and which Gordon accompanied, fared no better. Many shared Gordon's opinion, expressed in a letter written after the fall of the Mamelon : " I do not think the place can hold out for another ten days, and Sevastopol once taken, the Crimea is ours." The Russian defence was more stubborn than the most competent judges had expected; technically, Sevastopol was never taken, and, since the Russians held the north shore till peace was signed, the Crimea was never ours. Although our people did not achieve the Redan on the day the Mamelon fell, they were successful in seizing and holding the important position of the " Quarries," in front of it ; and Gordon bore his share in the enterprise, escaping, more fortunate than many gallant comrades, without a scratch. Here is an extract from a letter written by his brother :—" Only a few lines to say Charlie is all right, and has escaped amidst a terrific shower of grape and shells of all descriptions. You may imagine the suspense I was kept in until assured of his safety. He cannot write himself, and is now fast asleep in his tent, having been in the trenches from 2 o'clock yesterday morning during the can-

nonade until seven last night, and again from
12.30 this morning until noon."

The final bombardment began on September
5th; on the 8th the French took the Malakoff,
while we were unsuccessful in getting and keeping a firm grip on the Redan. A second
assault on that position was resolved on for the
following day, but it was not necessary to de-
liver it. The Russians evacuated Sevastopol
on the night between 8th and 9th September,
and withdrew across the harbour to the north
shore position. Gordon was for duty in the
trenches on the morning of the 9th, and this is
his account of what he saw :—" During the night
of the 8th I had heard terrific explosions, and
going down to the trenches at four next morning, I saw a splendid sight. The whole of
Sevastopol was in flames, and every now and
then terrible explosions took place, while the ris-
ing sun shining on the place had a most beautiful
effect. The Russians were leaving the town by
the bridge ; all the three deckers were sunk, the
steamers alone remaining. Tons and tons of
powder must have been blown up. About eight
o'clock I got an order to commence a plan of
the works, for which purpose I went to the

Redan, where a dreadful sight was presented. The dead were buried in the ditch—the Russians with the English—Mr. Wright reading the burial service over them."

Gordon went on duty with the expedition to Kinburn, and participated in the reduction of that place; after which he returned to the Crimea, where he remained until the evacuation in February, 1856, engaged in the duty, so distasteful to an engineer, of demolishing the defences, arsenal, and dockyard of the fallen stronghold. Mr. Hake quotes some letters written home by Gordon, chiefly between the third bombardment and the final stroke of good fortune. What is, characteristic in these may be extracted here. Gordon clearly, and with justice, had a high respect for the soldierhood of the Russians; and perhaps his idiosyncracy did not allow him to do adequate justice to the French. "The Russians," says he, "are brave, better I think than the French, who begin to fear them." Again, "the Russians certainly are inferior to none; their work is stupendous, and their shell practice beautiful." And yet again, on June 15th, "the Russians are downhearted though determined; they are much to be admired, and their officers are quite as cool as our officers under fire."

He thus refers to Lord Raglan's death and character :—"Lord Raglan died of tear and wear and general debility. He was universally regretted, as he was so kind. His life has been entirely spent in the service of his country. I hope he was prepared, but do not know." The last sentence indicates what ever has been uppermost in Gordon's thoughts. Writing previously of the sudden end of Captain Craigie, a brother officer, he says, " I am glad to say that he was a serious man. The shell burst above him, and by what is called chance, struck him in the back, killing him at once." It is by such utterances that the reader can form for himself a better conception of the tenets of this remarkable man, than could be conveyed in pages of attempted characterisation ; a man's own words, especially when they are not intended for effect, give the truest tracing of his mental and moral lineaments. On August 3rd he writes, "We are disappointed that General Jones did not mention Brown in the attack on the Quarries." This is the *esprit de corps;* but he goes on to guard himself individually against an appetite for mili-

c

tary glory—" I, for one," he adds, " do not care
about being 'lamented' after death." If he
comments on neglect, it is no personal growl—
" I am not ambitious," he says, "but what easily
earned C.B.'s and Majorities there are in some
cases! while men who have earned them, like
poor Oldfield, get nothing.   I am sorry for him.
He was always squabbling about his batteries
with us, but he got more done by his perseverance than any man before did."

The close of the Crimean War saw Gordon's
status defined among his comrades and superiors as an officer of adequate parts and of
sterling trustworthiness.   He had no opportunities to give earnest of his great future, but
as Chesney has recorded, his "special aptitude
for war" had been recognized by the men who
had the best means of forming the judgment.
Sir Harry Jones reported of him as an officer
who had done gallant service, and indicated that
he had earned promotion, if the regulations of
his corps had permitted that advancement.
And he was awarded the Legion of Honour, a
token of distinction conferred on few officers of
his rank, for as yet he was a subaltern.   His
promotion as first lieutenant had come to him

in February, 1855, just as he began his trench
work, but he was not to get his captaincy until
three years after the Crimean War had ended.

By the Treaty of Paris Russia lost what she
has since regained by the Treaty of Berlin in
1878, a slice of territory the possession of which
carries with it a control over the lower Danube.
Until 1812 this territory had been part of the
Turkish Empire, when it fell to Russia among
the spoils of Kutusoff's successful campaign. By
the Treaty of Bucharest Russian Bessarabia had
been advanced to the Pruth, and the principality
of Moldavia proportionately curtailed. Now
there was to be the retrocession to Moldavia of
what had been taken from it forty-five years
before. A commission, consisting of English,
French, Russian, and Austrian officers, was
appointed to lay down the new frontier line,
and the British commissioner was Major
Stanton (now Sir Edward Stanton). Lieutenants Gordon and James, both engineers, as
was their principal, were assistant commissioners, and their duties began in the summer
of 1856. There was plenty of variety in the
work. If the salt marshes bordering the Black
Sea are detestable and noxious, if life about the

Kilia mouth of the Danube is amphibious, and
presents the added joy of mosquitoes whose
size and viciousness are only to be found
equalled in Manitoba, if Kischeneff, the headquarters of the commission, was and is one of
the most commonplace, sordid, and unattractive
of the huge villages which in Southern Russia
pass for towns ; there was life and colour and
picturesqueness in the quaint semi-oriental
towns of the Principality. Jassy, the Moldavian
capital, thirty years ago was even a quainter
field for ethnological study than it is to-day.
Ismail, on the Danube, still then showed in its
shattered walls the print of Potemkin's furious
attacks, and the not less memorable stubborn-
ness of its defence. Gordon and James "rode
the marches" for nearly a year, verifying or
correcting the Russian maps, surveying the
boundary line, and carrying despatches. We
are told that Gordon, in this work, so different
from that in which he had been engaged in the
Crimea, enjoyed himself greatly, and took a
keen interest in all that he saw. It was finished
at length, after multitudinous disputes, for the
Russians begrudged the surrender ; but Gordon
was not free to return to England. He was

ordered instead, to transfer himself to similar work in another continent. There was a delimitation commission in Asia Minor as well as in Bessarabia, at the head of which Colonel Simmons (now Sir Lintorn Simmons) was engaged. Him Gordon was ordered to join. Gordon was home-sick, and telegraphed to solicit that another officer might be substituted. But he was a proven useful man, and the peremptory answer came back, " Lieutenant Gordon must go." In Armenia he first came into contact with wild uncivilised peoples, and learned to understand their complex yet simple nature. His duties on the commission took him to the historic places of the land so teeming with associations, and he ascended Mount Ararat. Mr. Hake writes, "After six months spent in these regions he went back to Constantinople, to be present at a conference of the commission. Here he remained longer than he had expected, to nurse his chief, who had fallen ill. This done, he was not sorry to return to England after his three years' absence. Another six months in England, and he was once more sent to Armenia as commissioner. Here he remained from the spring of 1858 until nearly the end of the year, employed in verifying the frontier he had taken so active a part in laying down, and in examining the new road between the Russian and Turkish dominions."

After his return to England from this frontier delimitation service, Gordon had a turn of "duty soldiering" at home, in the capacity of Instructor of Fieldworks and Adjutant at Chatham. He attained the rank of Captain on April 1st, 1859. He had then been a soldier for seven years, less two months. His age was twenty-six.

CHAPTER II.

LEAVING England for China in July, 1860, Captain Gordon did not reach the scene of our military operations there in time to participate in the capture of the Taku Forts. But September saw him at Tientsin, whence the allied forces had already commenced (September 9) their advance on Pekin, since the Chinese Commissioners were shuffling in the Chinese manner in regard to compliance with the conditions on which the allies were prepared to suspend hostilities and conclude peace. It was in the course of this movement, while negotiations were still proceeding, and had suddenly seemed prospering when indeed a basis of arrangement had been agreed to, that the representatives of the British Ambassador with their escort, while on their way back to the army from Tungchow after a not unsatisfactory conference with the

Chinese Commissioners, were beset, made prisoners, vilely maltreated, and finally carried off to
dungeons in Pekin, whence few of the party
emerged alive. This outrage made further negotiations out of the question until satisfaction had
been exacted. Lord Elgin informed the Chinese
authorities that he would sign no convention
with the Imperial Commissioners except within
the walls of Pekin ; and the stern pronounce-
ment was made good. But as the advance was
now to be an avowedly hostile one, certain additional military preparations had to be made
which detained the allied armies near Tungchow
until the beginning of October. This pause
gave Captain Gordon the opportunity of joining
the British force which the late Sir Hope Grant
so ably commanded. Pekin was reached on
6th October, and during the two following days
the army confronted the north wall of the capital,
with the principal concentration directed against
the An-ting Gate.

The allied commanders had given the Chinese
authorities until noon on the 13th to surrender
the gate, failing which immediate hostile action
would be resorted to. The artillery and engineers were in possession of a temple close to the

gate, and under cover of its courtyard were busying themselves in getting the siege train ready for action. In this work Gordon participated. "We were sent down," he writes, "in a great hurry to throw up works and batteries against the town, as the Chinese refused to give up the gate we required them to surrender before we would treat with them. The Chinese were given until noon, on the 13th (October) to give up the (An-ting) gate. We made a lot of batteries, and everything was ready for the assault of the wall, which is battlemented, and forty feet high, but of inferior masonry. At 11.30 p.m. (12th), however, the gate was opened, and we took possession, so our work was of no avail." It became a problem for Lord Elgin, in what manner to inflict an adequate punishment for the treacherous seizure of Parkes and his companions, the murders wrought on so many of the party, and the diabolical cruelty inflicted on all its members. To burn the capital would have been to punish a vast population guiltless of complicity in the outrage. Yet the penalty had to be one that would ring throughout the whole empire. The complicity of the Emperor and the Government in the treatment of the prisoners stood proven. These had been taken in the first instance to the Yuen-Ming-Yuen, the celebrated "Summer Palace," and there had been begun the ill-usage which resulted in so many deaths. The clothing of the victims had been found in the palace, and their horses in the imperial stables. So the orders were given for the destruction of the "Summer Palace" by fire. The vast and costly bonfire was kindled on the 18th October, and during the whole of the next day Yuen-Ming-Yuen was still burning; the clouds of smoke, driven by the wind, hung like a vast pall over Pekin. Next day Prince Yung intimated absolute submission to all the demands of the allies, and four days later a treaty was signed with much pomp in the Hall of Ceremonies, around which bristled British bayonets in the very heart of the Imperial City. At this scene Gordon was not present, "as all officers commanding companies were obliged to remain in camp, owing to the ill-treatment the prisoners experienced at the Summer Palace." The men were vicious, and needed controlling from exacting revenge. But he saw, and deplores, the destruction of the "Summer Palace." He writes :—"We went out, and after pillaging it,

burned the whole place, destroying in a vandal-
like manner most valuable property, which could
not be replaced for four millions. We got upwards of £48 a piece as prize money; and
although I have not had as much as many, I
have done well. Imagine D—— giving 16s.
for a string of pearls, which he sold the next
day for £500! You can scarcely imagine the
beauty and magnificence of the places we burned.
It made one's heart sore to burn them ; in fact,
those palaces"—there was a great imperial settlement, upwards of 200 buildings, and the
grounds covered an area of eight by ten miles
in extent—" were so large, and we were so
pressed for time, that we could not plunder
them carefully. Quantities of gold ornaments
were burned, considered as brass. It was
wretchedly demoralising work for an army.
Everybody was wild for plunder. . . You would
scarcely conceive the magnificence of this residence, or the tremendous devastation the French
have committed. The throne and room were
lined with ebony, carved in a marvellous way.
There were huge mirrors of all shapes and
kinds, clocks, watches, musical boxes with pup-
pets on them, magnificent china of every de-

scription, heaps and heaps of silks of all colours, embroidery, and as much splendour and civilization as you would see at Windsor; carved ivory screens, coral screens, large amounts of treasure, &c. The French have smashed everything in the most wanton way. It was a scene of utter destruction, which passes my description."

Gordon accompanied Sir Hope Grant's force on its retirement to Tientsin in November, where it went into winter quarters. Headquarters moved from the Peiho in the following year, but a detachment of British troops was left, and Gordon remained at Tientsin until the spring of 1862, in the capacity of officer commanding the Royal Engineers. From Tientsin during this period of comparative quiet, he made numerous journeys into the surrounding country, and in one of those rides he and his companion, Lieutenant Cardew, were able to accomplish the enterprise of exploring a considerable section of the " Great Wall of China." It was an adventurous journey, for they penetrated into districts where no " Foreign Devil " had been before them, and on one occasion they had to ride for their lives. Their servant and interpreter was a Chinese lad who knew some "pigeon" English, and their baggage was carried in a couple of carts. At Kalgan they found the wall, with its parapet, twenty-two feet high, and sixteen broad, the faces of huge bricks, and the interior filled with rubble. From Kalgan they followed the lines of the wall west to Taitung, where the wall was not so high, and where they saw the camel caravans, laden with "brick tea," on the route to Siberia. Fetching a wide south-westerly circuit in exploration of the line of the inner wall, and looking for a road eastward through the mountains flanking the Peiho basin on the north, they ultimately struck the thoroughfare at Taiyuen. Here they got into trouble for the first and only time. Dr. Birkbeck Hill tells the story. "When their bill was brought them for their night's lodgings they found the charge enormous. Seeing that a dispute would arise, they sent on their carts, and waited at the inn till they felt sure these had got well on their way. Then they offered what they thought was a reasonable sum. It was refused. They tried to mount their horses, but the people of the inn stopped them. Captain Gordon took out his revolver, for show more than for use, for he allowed them to take it from him. Then he said, 'Let us go to the Mandarin.' To this they agreed, and gave him back his revolver. They all walked toward the Mandarin's house—the two Englishmen along- side their horses. On the way Captain Gor- don said to his companion, 'Are you ready to mount?' 'Yes,' answered Cardew; so they mounted quietly, and went on with the people. When they reached the Mandarin's they turned their horses, and scampered after their carts as fast as they could. The people yelled and rushed after them, but it was too late." So, in cold so intense that "raw eggs were frozen hard as if they had been boiled," they crossed the mountains, and, after sundry vicissitudes, finally reached Tientsin more than fourteen days after their leave had expired.

This journey, which occupied two months, was made in the winter 1861-2, and in May of the latter year Gordon, with some infantry details, was ordered to Shanghai, in the vicinity of which the Tai-ping rebels were becoming so aggressive that it was considered requisite by Sir Charles Staveley, who now commanded the English forces in China, to operate against

them. Gordon now found himself in that
Kiangnan district which was later the scene of
his wonderful exploits at the head of the " Ever
Victorious Army." It is impossible, in the
narrow limits of this work, to give a detailed
narrative of the origin and progress of that
strange uprising the Tai-ping Rebellion. It
had been raging with varied fortune for twelve
years when Gordon was appointed to the task
of confronting and quelling it, and there are few
histories covering so short a space of time, that
are fuller charged with sensational incident. A
brief summary, nevertheless, is absolutely essen-
tial to the understanding of the events that
occurred in the fourteen final months during
which Gordon hammered at the Rebellion until
he broke it.

Between " the Heavenly King " of the Tai-
ping Rebellion, and " the Mahdi " of the Soudan, there is a certain analogy which probably
has occurred to Gordon long before now. Both
are of the people. Hung Sew-tsuen was " a
poor youth of a rude, despised race ; " Mohammed Ahmed is the son of a Dongola carpenter. Both professed, and perhaps felt religious enthusiasm ; both certainly made a

weapon of the religious enthusiasm with which
they were able to inspire masses. The character of neither displays personal heroism; both
schemed and allowed others to fight their
battles. Both characters are full of personal
licentiousness and ruthless cruelty; the Mahdi's
"indiscriminate executions" in Obeid, and his
eighteen wives, find some parallel in the
Heavenly King's "exterminating decrees," and
his harem indulgences in Nanking. It has
befallen Charles Gordon to cope with both.
Will their fates be similar? We know how
the "Heavenly King" came by his end; will
the career of the Mahdi parallel his down to its
violent close?

In the earlier days of China, Hung Sew-tsuen
might not even have expanded into a "village
Hampden," but might have grumbled his life
through as a peasant lad of the Hakkas,
the rude hill race to which he belonged—
the "Strangers"—who are regarded by the
"Punti" or "In-dwellers" of the Kwangtung
province, much, as Dr. Wilson expressively puts
it, "as the Irish of Liverpool are by the English
workmen of that city." Perhaps if he had
passed his examination at Canton he might

have merged into an official, and the Tai-ping Rebellion had never been. But he failed ; all the conditions of his life soured him ; and he began to think. The "Opium War" of 1841-2 had shaken the internal prestige of the Imperial Government, and a bold young fellow like this soured Hakka might even dare to sneer at the emblem of omnipotence in the person of a Mandarin. He would find around him in his clan people who had been carrying arms during the war, and had gained some glimmering notion of the might of the sword. There was a stirring of the dry bones of the Chinese Empire, and this young schoolmaster was first the creature and then the compeller of the movement. He invented a religion — from Mahomet to Te Whiti, that has been the grand leverage to move races,—and into the mosaic of which this new religion of his was composed, he worked a grim and distorted caricature of Christianity. He had possessed himself of the material he used in this way by having, in 1847, sat at the feet of an uneducated American mis-sionary whom he found working in Canton. He turned this simple man inside out, and took away of the product just what suited himself.

D

Dr. Wilson holds this undoubtedly remarkable Hakka man to have been far from a mere cunning impostor. "To the grossly superstitious Hakka, and to the ardent student of the more ancient Chinese classics, there was now added," he writes, "a third person, so to speak, imbued with certain Hebrew and Christian beliefs. It is a proof of the extraordinary power of this man's mind, and the depth of his convictions, that he could blend these three individuals so completely into one under the transmuting belief in his own mission. These results were far above the power of a mere cunning impostor. From the hour when Hung arose from his sick bed, after his first forty days' trance, and, poor and nameless, proclaimed his ovation by fixing on his door-post the proclamation, 'The noble principles of the Heavenly King, the Sovereign King Tsuen,' and through success and defeat and imperial opposition, up to the hour of his death in Nanking, he seems never to have wavered or abated one jot of his claim to supreme rule on earth." Most of us now, it may be supposed, are rather inclined to take Chesney's view that Hung was an able, astute, and keen-sighted impostor. Since in the jargon of his pretended visions there were some traces of his New Testament study, he had the singular fortune—this being of blood and lust— to find sympathy among good and fervent people here in England, who were fain to recognise in him a man who had put his hand to the enterprise of evangelising the East. The controversy is long dead and forgotten ; there may be said that there is *primâ facie* evidence that Gordon regarded the Heavenly King as an impostor, in virtue of his acceptance of the conduct of operations against him.

The Hakka schoolmaster proclaimed his "mission" in 1850. A vast horde gathered to him. He nominated five "Wangs" or soldier sub-kings from out his clan, and commenced his northward movement from Woosewen in January, 1851. Through the rich prosperous provinces his desultory march, interspersed with frequent halts, spread destruction and desolation. The peaceful fled shudderingly before this wave of fierce stalwart ruffianhood, with its tatterdemalian tawdriness, its flaunting banners, its rusty naked weapons. Everywhere it gathered in the local scoundrelism. The pirates came from the coast ; the robbers from

the interior mountains rallied to an enterprise
that promised so well for their trade. In the
perturbed state of the Chinese population the
horde grew like an avalanche as it rolled along.
The Heavenly King met with no opposition to
speak of, and in 1853 his promenade ended under
the shadow of the Porcelain Tower, in the city
of Nanking, the second metropolis of the Chinese
Empire, where till the rebellion and his life
ended simultaneously he lived a life of licentiousness, darkened further by the grossest cruelties.

The rebellion had lasted nearly ten years
when the fates brought it into collision with the
armed civilization of the West. The Imperialist
forces had made sluggishly some head against
it. Nanking had been invested after a fashion
for years on end. " The prospects of the Tai-
pings," says Commander Brine, " in the early
spring of 1860 had become very gloomy." The
Imperialist generals had hemmed Tai-pingdom
within certain limits in the lower valley of the
Yantsze, and the movement languished further
" from its destructive and exhausting nature,
which for continued vitality constantly required
new districts of country to exhaust and destroy."

But in 1859 China and the West came into

collision. Admiral Hope failed to force the passage of the Peiho. The Imperial Government knew something by this time of the British character, and knowing what was before it, concentrated much of its attention in strengthening further the defences of that river. The subjugation of the Tai-pings ceased to be a prime object, and the rebellion had opportunity to recover lost ground. For the sixth time the "Faithful King" relieved Nanking. The Imperialist generals fell back, and then the Tai-pings took the offensive, and as the result of sundry victories, the rebellion regained an active and flourishing condition. In 1860 the Faithful King was free to march into the rich district of Yiangnan, the chief city of which, Soochow, he entered almost without opposition. Shanghai, one of the treaty ports, was threatened, but there was in Shanghai a force of allied English and French troops, who when the Tai-pings attempted the place drove them back with heavy loss. The Kiangnan district continued to be held by large Tai-ping forces, but in the beginning of 1861 Admiral Hope, in the course of a voyage up the Yangtsze, visited Nanking, and there entered into an arrangement with the Heavenly

King who held his court there, that the river
trade was not to be interfered with nor Shanghai
to be molested by the Tai-ping forces, for the
space of one year.   This convention was kept;
but in the face of warnings from the Admiral,
the Heavenly King ordered his general, immediately on its expiry, to move on Shanghai.
The Faithful King advanced from Soochow in
the early part of 1862, proclaiming, "We must
take Shanghai to complete our dominions," and
heralding his advent by the smoke of burning
villages.   Now for the first time did the allies
take the field against the Tai-pings; and this
solely to secure the safety of Shanghai.   Sir
Charles Staveley, who had succeeded to the
command of the British forces, considered that
this could best be effected by maintaining
around that city a clear radius of thirty miles.
At first the allied forces which he commanded,
in conjunction with the Imperialist levies, had
fair success, but reverses occurred, and until the
Faithful King was summoned by his master to
Nanking, the Tai-pings held and laid waste the
country up to the city walls.

It was to assist in the operations Staveley
was engaging in that Captain Gordon was

summoned from the Peiho to Shanghai, in May,
1862. He was Commanding Engineer, and
had a prominent position in the conduct of
affairs. He was in command at the storm of
Singpoo, and in October of the same year he was
with the force which cleared the rebels out of
Kading, one of the places Staveley had abandoned in the earlier part of the year. One of
his letters about this time makes reference to
the Tai-ping character. "We had a visit,"
says he, "from the marauding Tai-pings the
other day. They came close down in small
parties to the settlement, and burnt several
houses, driving in thousands of inhabitants.
We went against them and drove them away,
but did not kill many. They beat us into fits
in getting over the country, which is intersected
in every way with ditches, swamps, &c. . . . .
You can scarcely conceive the crowd of peasants
who come into Shanghai when the rebels are in
the neighbourhood—upwards of 15,000 I should
think, and of every size and age—many strapping fellows who could easily defend themselves
come running in with old women and children.
. . . . The people on the confines are suffering
greatly, and are in fact dying of starvation. It

is most sad, this state of affairs, and our Government really ought to put the rebellion down. Words could not depict the horrors these people suffer from the rebels, or describe the utter deserts they have made of this rich province."

When the Faithful King's withdrawal gave comparative and temporary peace to the region around Shanghai, Gordon was engaged on the survey of the thirty miles radius around that city, and the conversance he thus gained of the complicated amphibious country, was to stand him in valuable stead a little later. "I have been now," he writes, "in every town and village in the thirty mile radius. . . . . The country is the same everywhere, a dead flat with innumerable creeks and bad pathways." *L'homme propose*—Gordon believed that it was all over; "the people," he continues, "have now settled down quiet again, and I do not anticipate the rebels will ever come back; they are rapidly on the decline, and two years ought to bring about the utter suppression of the revolt." The revolt was suppressed, it is true, in less than two years, but when Gordon wrote the last sentence, he certainly had no notion that there could be so venomous a sting in its tail.

When, in 1860, Shanghai was threatened by
the Tai-ping forces that had pervaded and conquered the district of Kiangnan, a number of
wealthy merchants of that commercial city determined to subscribe funds for the establish-
ment of a foreign force for the purpose of
checking the enterprising enemy. A couple of
Americans, whose names were Ward and Burgevine, were engaged to recruit and organise this
force, of which Ward was to have the command.
Ward was an adventurer and a seaman ; but he
had useful military instincts, he was a man of
great personal bravery, and his character commanded respect. He and his followers did a
good deal of hard fighting, with chequered
fortunes, between 1860 and 1862. Ward had
been filling his ranks by disciplining Chinese, and
the force he commanded fought so well in the
operations of the early part of the latter year,
in co-operation with the allied troops of the
Shanghai garrison, that it began to be known
by the title of the " Ever Victorious Army "—a
title that soon was to become so familiar to the
world. Later a detachment of the " False
Foreign Devils," as Ward's soldiers were called
by the Tai-pings, because, although Chinese, he

dressed them in European clothes, sustained a
serious reverse at Singpoo, and Colonel For-
rester, its commander, was made a prisoner.
Ward participated with part of his force in the
operations conducted by Captain Roderick Dew,
R.N., against the Tai-pings in the vicinity of
Ningpo, in the region south of Hangchow Bay,
and was killed by a chance ball during the
escalade of the town of Tseki. Dr. Wilson
says of him : "So passed away a man who, as
the originator of the idea of disciplining the
Chinese, had done good service. Surmounting
all difficulties, Ward had gained a strange as-
cendancy over Europeans, as well as Chinese,
by his cool and daring courage. Ever foremost
in fight, he was honourably scarred ; but his
ambition was boundless ; and perhaps it was
well for the Imperial Government of China that
he was removed at this stage of the Rebellion,
and that his work was left to be completed by
one who, though his equal in courage and in
coolness, far surpassed him in all the higher
qualities of a soldier." Soon after his death,
his force went back to Shanghai, Captain Dew
not sorry to end the connection, for Ward's
men robbed and " squeezed " with great industry.

Ward's second in command, Colonel For-
rester, declined to succeed him in the command
of the "Ever Victorious Army," and the position fell to Burgevine, a more unscrupulous
soldier of fortune than had been his prede-
cessor. He soon came to loggerheads with Li-
Hung-Chang, the Imperialist Governor-General
of the Kiang provinces—" Governor Li," as he
was known in England in those days. The
quarrel was intensified by a variety of circumstances, and in January, 1863, Burgevine was
dismissed. Li begged Sir Charles Staveley to
appoint a British officer to the vacant command.
Staveley entertained the request, but had to
refer to the Home Government for sanction
thus to dispose of the services of a British
officer. He recommended Gordon for the
appointment. Gordon was engaged in the
survey work of which mention has already
been made, and Mr. Hake says that he asked
permission to be allowed to finish that duty
before entering on the command offered him,
on the ground that the completed survey would
be of great service to him in the subsequent
military operations he would have to undertake.
To this request General Staveley acceded, and

meanwhile the temporary command of the
" Ever Victorious Army " was given to Captain
Holland, R.M., General Staveley's Chief of
Staff. That officer strove to utilise his opportunity by making an attack, in conjunction with
an Imperialist brigade, upon the town of Taitsan, held by the Tai-pings, but suffered a defeat, with the loss of some guns and many
officers and men. No more successful was
Major Brennan's expedition against Fushan,
and the prestige of the " Ever Victorious
Army " was at a serious discount, when sanction reached General Staveley to entrust a
British officer with its permanent command.
Gordon—by this time Major Gordon, for he
had received his brevet for his services of the
previous year—was summoned from his survey
work, and the " Ever Victorious Army " had
now a chief under whom it was to make good
its title to that appellation.

Gordon had just turned thirty—a young man,
truly, for a task so arduous. But men of his
stamp are not to be judged by their years. The
art of war, perhaps more than any other art,
demands experience in its successful practi-
tioners. But sometimes, although rarely, sol-

diers move to the front in whom an innate genius for war dispenses with the tuition of experience. Sheridan, when he sent Early "whirling up the Shenandoah Valley," had not Gordon's years when the latter took the command of the "Ever Victorious Army." Ranald Mackenzie at twenty-one, was pronounced by General Grant the finest Cavalry-Division Commander of the Union Armies. Skobeleff had conquered Khokand before he reached eight-and-twenty. To cite a more illustrious example, Napoleon was but twenty-seven when he carried the Bridge of Lodi. Gordon was in the prime of mental and physical vigour. He had been a constant student of the art military; his nature was at once enterprising and cautious; he seemed to control his fellowmen by an intuitive influence; and the buoyancy of his temperament sustained him in every situation.

In what spirit he accepted the onerous task, an excerpt from a home letter will show, written in March, 1863. "I have taken the step on consideration. I think that any one who contributes to putting down this rebellion fulfils a humane task, and, I also think, tends a great deal to open China to civilisation. I will not act rashly, and I trust soon to be able to return to England. . . . I can say that if I had not accepted the command I believe the force would have broken up, and the rebellion gone on in its misery for years. I trust this will not now be the case. . . . I think I am doing a good service."

Something must be told of the constitution of the army whose command he took over in its headquarters at Sung-kiang. Its strength varied, while he had it, from 3,000 to 5,000 men, under about 150 officers. When he took it over, the private soldiers were mostly locally recruited, and were inferior to the Tai-pings both in physique and courage ; but Gordon almost at once began the practice of enlisting picked men from out the captured rebels, who, having been accustomed to hard work and no pay, found the new service an elysium, and who, taken to-day, had no objection to go into action against their late comrades to-morrow. The pay was good, and fairly regular, and the force was rationed, besides, when in the field. Discipline was as firm as might be, but there was little crime, and therefore few punishments. The infantry armament consisted of smooth-bore

English muskets, but one regiment had rifles, and three hundred Enfields were distributed to marksmen. " Every regiment," writes an ex-officer of the force, " could go through the manual and platoon and bayonet exercises to English words of command with a smartness and precision to which not many volunteer regiments can attain ; could manœuvre very fairly in companies or as a battalion, and each regiment had been put through a regular course of musketry instruction, the scores and returns being satisfactorily kept, and the good shots rewarded." But this must have held good only of the original levies. The artillery arm was exceptionally strong ; there were in all 52 pieces, most of large calibre, but nearly all mounted on travelling carriages. The building of batteries against fortified places was not resorted to, but the gunners were covered from musket and gingall fire by large wooden mantlets. There was a pontoon train for the larger rivers, and the force carried planks for bridging the creeks wherewith the country was intersected.

The non-commissioned officers were all Chinese, selected from the ranks ; but the commissioned officers were exclusively foreigners, and a most miscellaneous lot they were—as varied in origin as the officers of the Begum Sumroo's army, whose tombstones at Sirdhana record almost every European nationality. Americans were in the majority, but there were Englishmen, Germans, Frenchmen, Spaniards, Italians, Poles, and Greeks. Some were ex-mates of merchant ships, some old soldiers (rankers) of good character, some adventurers and refugees of no character at all. In one month, eleven officers died of *delirium tremens.* " There was no picking and choosing "—wrote one who had been in the force—" the general was too glad to get any foreigners to fill up vacancies, and the result, especially in garrison, was deplorable. They fought well, and led their men well, however, and that, after all, was the chief requisite." Chesney thus speaks of them—" Among them were avowed sympa-thisers with the rebels, and avowed defiers of Chinese law ; but all classes soon learnt to re-spect a general in whose kindness, valour, skill, and justice they found cause unhesitatingly to confide ; who never spared himself personal exposure when personal danger was near ; and beneath whose firm touch sank into insignifi-

cance the furious quarrels and personal jealou-
sies which had hitherto marred the usefulness of
the force."

Something must be told of the geography
and character of the region in which Gordon
led his army to thirty-three engagements in less
than two years. The theatre of his operations
was the district of Kiangnan, lying between the
lower portion of the Yantsze's course, its
northern boundary, and the deep, narrow bay
of Hangchow on the south. The width of the
blunt peninsula so formed, from Nanking on the
Yantsze, the Heavenly King's residence, to
Hangchow, at the head of the bay of the same
name, is about 150 miles ; its length from a line
drawn between these two places to where the
ocean bounds it, is about 200. Some twenty-
five miles inland from its extreme eastern apex,
on one of the innumerable creeks which thread
the region, lies the great treaty port of Shanghai. Densely peopled, thickly studded with
villages and towns, intersected in every direction by rivers, creeks, and canals, Kiangnan,
save for a few low isolated hills, is a dead level
teeming with fertility, never more than a few
feet above sea level, and occasionally actually

E

below that. Look across any portion of this vast plain, and boats, with mat sails spread, seem to be moving in every direction over the land. In warfare in such a country,—a vast network of canals and towpaths, where there are absolutely no roads, where wheeled vehicles are never used, and where the bridges still remaining were scarce and precarious, Gordon's survey experiences were of incalculable use. It was an immense advantage to know what canals were still. navigable, which choked with weeds ; where the ground would bear artillery, and where it was impassable swamp. " He knew," writes one of his officers, "every feature of the country better than any other person, native or foreigner, better even than the rebels who had been in partial possession for years." And he strengthened his hand by the formation and use of a flotilla of armed steamers and gunboats, which in that water-intersected country, served both to cover and flank all his movements, and also by swiftly transferring the force from one point to another, to multiply it to the enemy's imagination.

An Imperialist army co-operated with the force Gordon commanded, and his coadjutor-general was a Mandarin named Li Adong, a man whom he regarded as well fitted for his position and likely to be of great service. But Gordon, on assuming command of the " Ever Victorious Army," distinctly stipulated, and it was definitely arranged, that the discipline of that force and the appointment of its officers should be wholly vested in himself, and that the Chinese generals should have no power to hamper his movements. The Imperialist Governor-General was a shrewd, clear-headed man, who discerned what manner of man was this young officer of Engineers. He generally gave him full liberty of independent action ; he was mostly ready with support when it was asked for, and save in one instance he behaved towards Gordon with a confidence and loyalty which were rare in a Chinaman.

It was on March 25th, 1863, that Major Gordon reached Sung-kiang and took over the command of the " Ever Victorious Army "— then not quite in accord with its title, from Captain Holland. His staff consisted of Captain Stack, 67th Foot, as his chief of staff; Ensign Stevens, 99th Regiment, Adjutant-General ; Mr. Cooksley (of the Commissariat

Service), Quartermaster-General ; Lieutenant Ward, R.A., commanding Field Artillery; and Dr. Moffit, 67th Regiment, as P. M. O. He had to establish his position at the outset, for the force favoured Burgevine, but his tact carried him through this initial trouble. He convened the officers and noncommissioned officers, had some talk with them, and all was well for the time.

Then he busied himself with swift preparations for the immediate and energetic offensive, as being sure to prove the best defensive. He might have entered on deliberate and connected operations in co-operation with the Chinese troops. He might have contented himself with covering Shanghai, and perhaps nibbling the Tai-pings gradually out of the thirty miles radius round that place. But these were not tactics that recommended themselves to a man of Gordon's nature. He resolved on a quick sudden blow at a distant point, at once to confuse the enemy, to brace the despondent Imperialists, give heart and cohesion to his followers, and inspire them with confidence in their new chief. Where should he strike first ?

Seventy miles north-west of Shanghai, on the southern shore of the Yantsze estuary, is situated the town of Fushan, a pirate den, which the Tai-pings now held in some force, and had repulsed an attempt made to reduce it a short time before. Ten miles inland, but shut in by Fushan from access to the river, the town of Chanzu was holding out, lest worse things should befall the beleaguered garrison. For originally the commandant and soldiers of it had been themselves Tai-pings, but had declared for the Imperialist cause, and for the renegades to surrender would probably have been death. But the Faithful King, who was besieging Chanzu, had offered terms to the soldiers of its garrison if they would rat back again to the Tai-ping side ; and the commandant, who no doubt felt his own head rather loose on his shoulders in the event of a surrender, had to take off the heads of a considerable number of his soldiers to discourage the others from accepting the Faithful King's overtures.

On the enterprise of relieving Chanzu, Gordon, a few days after his assumption of command, was on his way from Sung-kiang,

with two steamer-loads of his infantry and
adequate artillery. Landing without opposition, under cover of an Imperialist force lying
entrenched near Fushan, he moved directly on
· that place. He planted his guns under cover
of night, breached the defences next morning
(April 14), after a three hours' bombardment ;
and the defenders did not wait to receive the
assault, but evacuated the place. Receiving
reinforcements from the direction of Chanzu,
they made a partial rally, but next morning
had abandoned all their positions, and were in
full retreat on Soochow. Fushan, Gordon's
first coup, was won at the cost of but two killed
and six wounded, but one of the former was
an English captain, named Belcher. Gordon
promptly marched to the relief of Chanzu,
passing on the way the corpses of thirty-five
Imperialist soldiers, first partially burnt, and
then crucified ; a spectacle which testified that
the tenacity of the Chanzu Governor had been
a wise discretion. The Tai-ping retreat had
opened the place, aud the population received
their deliverer with rejoicing. The Mandarins
gave Gordon and his officers a state reception,
and he has recorded his impressions of the

ci-devant rebel officers :—" I saw," says he, " the young rebel chiefs who had come over ; they are very intelligent and splendidly dressed, with big pearls in their caps. The head man is about thirty-five years old ; he looked worn to a thread with anxiety. He was so very glad to see me, and chin-chinned most violently, regretting his inability to give me a present, which I told him was not the custom with us people."

Having executed his purpose thus brilliantly, and leaving 300 of his men in garrison at Fushan, he returned to his headquarters at Sung-kiang, and devoted himself for the moment to improve the condition and discipline of his force, and prepare himself for a vigorous campaign. Burgevine had been intriguing up at Pekin ; but Governor Li settled his pretensions in a report to his official superior, an extract from which deserves quotation.

" As the people and the place are charmed with him (Gordon), as he has already given me returns of the organisation of the force, the formation of each regiment, and the expenses ; as he wishes to drill our troops and save our money; as it is evident that he fully comprehends the state of affairs ; and as in the expedition he is preparing his men delightedly obey him and preserve the proper order ; I cannot therefore remove him without due cause."

The expedition he was now preparing was a campaign which was to restore Kiangnan to the Imperial arms, and by breaking the neck of the rebellion, lead to the general pacification of China.

Gordon's plans and preparations were soon made, and already, before the close of April, he had commenced operations. The natural capital and central point of the theatre of the war was the great city of Soochow, which the Tai-pings had held ever since May, 1860. To regain it for the Imperial power may well be supposed to have been the keynote to Gordon's scheme of operations. But there offered a judicious alternative to a direct advance. About thirty-five miles north from Shanghai lies the walled town of Taitsan, held by the Tai-pings, and connected with Soochow by a main road running westward from Taitsan to Soochow, threading on its course, about midway, the important town of Quinsan. *A cheval* as it was on the line of communications between Taitsan and Soochow, Quinsan was obviously a place of immense strategical significance ; and further, it was the arsenal of the Tai-pings, where they had established a shot factory under some vagabond Englishmen. Quinsan, then, was Gordon's immediate objective. He was moving on that place, when he had suddenly to divert his force on Taitsan to inflict exemplary retribution for an act of the basest treachery. The Tai-ping commander of Taitsan had made proposals of surrender to Governor Li. These may have been simply a snare, or there may have been some reality originally in them, for Gordon's work at Fusan might well have intimidated the Taitsan commander. Anyhow, negotiations had gone on, and an Imperialist column was sent up by agreement to occupy the place. Presents had been interchanged, and the day had been fixed for the surrender. On that day a large detachment of the Imperialist force was actually admitted, when, at a signal, the gate was closed, and the detachment was treacherously attacked and seized. Three hundred were decapitated, and the heads sent to Soochow and Quinsan as an evidence of the smartness and fidelity of the Taitsan commander.

Gordon put aside his project of striking at Quinsan, and moved on Taitsàn with all speed, undeterred by the arduous character of the new enterprise. For Taitsan had a garrison of 10,000 men, 2,000 of whom were picked braves. The place was well found in artillery, and the gun detachments were officered by several English, French, and American adventurers in the Tai-ping employment. Coming upon the place from the south, he worked round to its west, keeping out of gunshot from the walls, and capturing some outworks that had covered the Quinsan road, cut off the communication in that direction. His heavy guns, with their mantlet protection, were pushed forward, and opened fire on the walls. On the second day of the bombardment, May 2nd, a practicable breach was achieved by their fire. A regiment had been moved toward the North Gate, at once to stop the retreat of the garrison, and to cover the left flank of the attacking force. The moat was bridged, and the stormers crossed to the assaults under the command of Captain Banning. But the Tai-pings, full of fight, manned the breach, engaged hand to hand with the assailants, and drove them back. Gordon, following the tactics of Grahame at San Sebastian, caused his artillery to play over the stormers' heads, and so cleared the breach. The forlorn hope again attacked, this time crowned the breach, and the colours of the victorious regiment waved from the top of the wall. The Tai-pings broke and fled in every direction, trampling each other to death in their eagerness to escape. Seven hundred Chinese prisoners, were made, and enlisted into the ranks of the Ever Victorious Army; the foreign mercenaries received scant mercy, and seven of them were killed. The loss of Gordon's force in the capture of Taitsan was not inconsiderable. Captain Banning and twenty men were killed; seven of his officers and 142 privates were wounded. A clamour raised that Gordon's army had been guilty of inhuman conduct, indeed of the " most refined cruelty," was refuted by him; and rebutted even more conclusively by General Brown, the officer in command of the British troops about Shanghai, who testified that the execution of seven Tai-pings—the circumstances of which formed the burden of the charge—was carried out by an independent Imperialist force lying six miles distant from Taitsan.

Gordon writes of the reduction of Taitsan :
" I attacked the two large stockades in one day
and the town on the next. The rebels made a
good fight, but it was no use, and the place fell.
. . . . Its capture opens out a large tract of
country, and the Chinese generals were delighted, and have said all manner of civil things
about the force. I am now a Tsung Ping
Mandarin (which is the second highest grade),
and have acquired a good deal of influence. I
do not care about that overmuch. I am quite
sure I was right in taking over the command,
as you would say, if you saw the ruthless
character of the rebels."

There had been plundering at Taitsan, and
some consequent demoralisation of the " Ever
Victorious Army ; " so Gordon took it back to
Sung-kiang for reorganization. Some of the
officers displayed a marked distaste for discipline, and Gordon was able to replace the most
disaffected by non-commissioned officers and
privates from the British regiments in Shanghai, whom General Brown had allowed to
volunteer. But he was never quite free from
the trouble of indiscipline among his officers.
Near the end of May he prepared to move on

Quinsan a second time. He found occasion to promote his Commissary-General, Cooksley, to the rank of Lieutenant-Colonel, so that he might have the right to exercise command over the majors who commanded the regiments. The latter took umbrage at this promotion, and claimed for themselves equal rank and pay. This refused, they sent in their resignations, with the anomalous demand that these should be at once accepted, but that they should be allowed to serve on the impending expedition. Gordon accepted their resignations, refusing the rider ; but he was marching out next morning ! When the " fall in " sounded, only his own body-guard obeyed ; and the officers who had been appointed in room of the majors reported that the men would not move. Finally the majors accepted the situation, and the force, consisting of 600 artillery and 2,300 infantry, marched on Quinsan, in assisting to assail which an Imperialist force under General Ching, was to co-operate. The key to all future operations against Soochow, reconnaissances and reports proved Quinsan to be in itself strong. The ditch around it was over 100 feet wide ; the approaches were

furnished with forts inside stockades ; the garrison was estimated at from 12,000 to 15,000
men.   How was it to be assailed ?   General
Ching was anxious that the attack should be
on the eastern side, that looking toward Taitsan.   But Gordon's military insight guided him
to another method.   In the issue, he virtually
took this great city with a little river steamboat.
It was an extraordinary exploit, and, if the description of it appeared in a novel, the writer
might be complimented on his inventive faculty,
but desired, another time, to adhere somewhat
closer to possibility.

Gordon discovered that the only land communication between Quinsan and Soochow was
by a single causeway, narrow in places, flanked
all the way by a canal, and that canal acces-
sible to his flotilla approaching it by a creek
from the south.   By seizing this causeway he
would cut the communication between the two
cities, and so the reinforcement of the Quinsan
garrison from as well as its retreat to Soochow
being hindered, he might deal with it presently
as circumstances should suggest.   On board
the " Hyson " he started on this romantic expedition, with a flotilla of sailing gunboats, which

carried, too, a picked but small infantry battalion armed with rifles. The "Hyson," which mounted a 32-pounder gun, and a 12-pound howitzer, was commanded by a rugged but valiant American skipper named Davidson, and craft and skipper had already made their names. She had the reputation of being amphibious—able to drive over the bed of a creek on her paddle-wheels, when there was not water enough to float her; he, man enough to fight the "Hyson" as if she had been a puissant ironclad. Chunye, about eight miles west from Quinsan, was the point at which Gordon's flotilla approached the causeway. The approach was protected by piles, which had to be pulled up, and by stockades on the land about the causeway, within which was a strong stone fort. This position he did not need to assault. A panic seized the defenders, and they bolted, a part running in upon Quinsan, the rest making along the causeway westward for Soochow. The troops were landed to occupy a position so important and so fortunately acquired, and the "Hyson" made a reconnaissance along the canal toward Soochow, her fire sweeping from the adjacent cause-

way and from the canal banks, alike detachments
on the march and those holding intermediate
stockaded positions. The little craft pushed
to within sight of Soochow, went about, and
returned toward Chunye. She was only just
in time. A desperate fight was raging in the
darkness on the causeway and its vicinity. The
garrison of Quinsan, scared by the tidings the
fugitives had brought in, and, since Gordon had
beset the town on the three other sides with his
own and Imperialist troops, in a panic lest their
means of retreat should utterly fail them, had
sallied out under cover of darkness, and were
heading along the causeway in the direction of
Soochow, when they encountered Gordon's
detachment commanding it at Chunye. To
this struggling, confused mêlée, the "Hyson"
came steaming through the darkness, her lights
ablaze, her steam whistle emitting demoniacal
yells—a mysterious, awe-inspiring monster. At
the sight a spasm of frantic terror seized the
hapless Tai-pings. They recoiled and drew
apart from the close struggle with Gordon's
men. Into them, thus huddled, tore the
fire from the steamer's foregun, and sent them
back on the beleaguered town a crazed mob of

fugitives. The Imperialists on the east side of the city marched in and took possession. Quinsan had fallen without having been assaulted.

Of its garrison eight hundred were taken, most of whom entered the ranks of the Ever Victorious Army. This was not a tithe of the garrison, nor did any great number ever succeed in reaching Soochow. The mass must have perished miserably in efforts to escape, drowned in creeks, smothered in mud, slaughtered by the villagers, who, infuriated by outrage, rose unanimously on the fugitives. This marvellous success Gordon had gained at a cost of two killed and five drowned. The fall of Quinsan gave him an admirable headquarter position—a central point communicating by water with Soochow, Sung-kiang, Taitsan, and Chanzu. And yet more, the boldness of the attack and the completeness of the success paralysed the Tai-pings and gave confidence to the country people.

But there ensued a double trouble. General Ching had been jealous of Gordon, and so resented his summary capture of Quinsan, an exploit he had himself been bent on achieving, that he not only quarrelled with Gordon, but fired, by

F

mistake as he alleged, into a detachment of the latter's force. Gordon moved into his vicinity to resent actively any further blunders of the same awkward description, but finally the affair terminated in a humble apology on Ching's part. While this affair was awaiting settlement Gordon had to cope with a more dangerous mutiny among his own troops than any that had previously occurred. The force had its connections at the old quarters in Sung-kiang, and was vehemently opposed to Quinsan as the new depôt station.

When the change was definitely ordered, the artillery refused to fall in, and threatened to blow the English officers to pieces with the big guns and the Chinese authorities with the small arms. A written proclamation of a sheer mutinous tenor was conveyed to Gordon. He paraded the non-commissioned officers, convinced that they were at the bottom of the mischief, and demanded to know who wrote the proclamation. They professed ignorance. "Then," rejoined Gordon, "I will shoot every fifth man of you." The gunner non-coms. replied with groans. The most vehement groaner, a corporal, Gordon dragged out of the rank and had him shot on the spot by two infantry men who were standing by. His comrades were locked up, told that if in one hour the writer's name was not given up, the threat of having every fifth man shot would be carried out. They gave in, the name was disclosed, and the mutiny was over. Another followed almost immediately after, this time among the commissioned officers of the artillery, who resented the promotion of Major Tapp to the command of that arm ; but Gordon's firmness quelled it also.

In a long letter home Gordon sketches his situation just after the capture of Quinsan ; some extracts may be made : " The rebels never got such a licking before, and I think there will not be much more severe fighting. My occupying this city enables the Imperial Government to protect an enormous district rich in corn, &c., and the people around are so thankful for their release that it is quite a pleasure. . . You may hear of cruelties being committed; do not believe them. We took nearly 800 prisoners, and they have some of them entered my body guard and fought since against their old friends the rebels. I took a Mandarin who had been a rebel for three years, and have him now ; he has a bullet in his cheek which he received in fighting against the rebels. . . The rebels Wangs or Kings knew that 'a new English *piecee* had come when Fushan was taken, but did not expect him at Taitsan.' Some of the reports spread are most amusing ; one is, that 'the rebels gave me £2000 not to attack Quinsan,' when I advanced on that place after the capture of Taitsan. All the mandarins have heard of this ; but it must have slightly upset their story when we came up again against Quinsan. I have four English officers with me ; we wear anything we can get, and the men are almost in rags. Having to move our headquarters (from Sung-kiang) has caused a good deal of work, and this is only just completed."

The next enterprise that presented itself was naturally the reduction of Soochow, the capital city of the province. Gordon believed that had the Imperialists' co-operation been possible, Soochow could have been rushed in the panic caused by the alarm of his cruise in the "Hyson." But now the undertaking had to be gone about systematically. The City of Pagodas is the centre of a great system of waterways, and can be reached on every side by water. Approaching it thus, then, Gordon resolved on isolating it by gradually mastering its communications and approaches. One main key to its approach on the south was the town of Kahpoo, ten miles south of it, and yet another was Wokong, three miles south again of Kahpoo. For the reduction of those places he quitted Quinsan with about 2200 men, artillery and infantry, and the armed steamers " Firefly," and " Cricket." Kahpoo he stormed on 27th April, and next day moved on Wokong so rapidly as to surprise some of the stockades outside which had been left un-guarded, and to carry others with little loss. A judicious disposition of his troops now enabled him to shut in the garrison of Wokong itself, and the Tai-pings surrendered. Four thousand prisoners were taken, among whom were many chief men. Of the prisoners, at his own urgent request, General Ching received some 1500 as recruits for his army, under strict promise that they should receive good treatment. But Ching broke his promise, for Gordon presently heard that five of these men had been beheaded. He was bitterly indignant at this breach of faith. There had been default, too, in the payment of his force, and this preyed heavily on his mind.

He had repressed plunder, using the argument
of regular pay ; now the regular pay was not
forthcoming, and his troops, having neither
"meal nor malt," plunder nor pay, were dis-
contented not without cause. Half of them had
deserted since Quinsan fell, and he had been
obliged to fill the gap with rebel prisoners.
But it was Ching's breach of faith, and his cause-
less cruelty, that filled Gordon's cup of dissatis-
faction with his position to overflowing. He
resolved to lay down his command and rode
down to Shanghai with that intent. But when
he 'reached that place on August 3rd, he found
that an event had occurred which caused him to
revoke his resolution. Burgevine had suddenly
left that place with some 300 European tag-rag
and bob-tail, to join the Tai-pings in Soochow,
carrying off a small steamer and throwing the
treaty port into a not unnatural fit of consterna-
tion. To abandon the Imperialist cause at such
a juncture was not to be thought of by Gordon,
for it would have been to have left his own
troops to be seduced from their allegiance by
their old commander, who had had the art to
impress them with the belief that his dismissal
had been the result of standing up for their rights.

Gordon at once started alone back to Quin-san. He must have had serious thoughts on that solitary night-ride, since so much hung on the temper of the officers whom he was to meet at dawn. He found appearances so bad, that he sent back his siege train to Taitsan, while reinforcing his advanced position at Kahpoo. He was attacked there in great force, and had a gunboat blown up, but beat off his assailants. Burgevine did not command the rebels in this attack; he was reported to be organising a foreign legion inside Soochow. Gordon during this period of defensive and anxiety writes home with perfect serenity : " The fact that Burgevine has joined the rebels will no doubt very much prolong the rebellion, which, humanly speaking, would almost have been put down this year, or at the latest, next spring, but the force at my command is too small in numbers to do every-thing, and one has to act with great caution in the changed aspect of affairs ; added to which is the idea the Imperialists have got into their heads that they can defeat the rebels in the field, which they cannot do. Many people urge me to attack, but my opinion is so much against it that their persuasion will be in vain for the

present. I feel I have so many lives entrusted
to me that these are, as it were, at my disposal,
and I will not risk them in an enterprise I
consider rash. Burgevine is a very foolish man,
and little thinks the immense misery he will
cause this unhappy country, for of the ultimate
suppression of the rebellion I have little doubt,
as it is a Government receiving revenues con-
tending with a faction almost blockaded, and
(that Government) commanding inexhaustible
sums. Burgevine's boy who has run out, says
he tells the Wangs all about the settlement and
the force, &c., which interests them very much.
He is in good health, but very indolent ; he has
a nice lot with him—all the scum of Shanghai,
which may be said to be celebrated for its pro-
duce in that way. He is not allowed to send
money down to Shanghai, so I expect the rebels
intend eventually to take it all back again. An
intercepted letter from Burgevine says he has
thirty or forty men who are with him who
declare they will run away at the first opportunity. I believe he now regrets his conduct
(in joining the rebels). Burgevine's agents
have been in vain trying to get my men over."
In a later letter, dated Sept. 25, written from

Waiquaidong, two miles east of Soochow, he mentions that Burgevine had been down in Shanghai, attempting to get arms there for the use of the rebels, had failed, and had narrowly escaped being captured.

There had been a great scare in Shanghai because of Burgevine's action in joining the rebels. It was notorious that Gordon's officers were not to be trusted. Indeed, there had come a report into the treaty port that Quinsan had been given up to the rebels by its garrison. The British commandant of Shanghai, writing to his military superior, let himself use such language as this : "Should this be true—the report just spoken of—the worst may be antici- pated ; Major Gordon a prisoner, the siege train lost, and the speedy advent of the rebels, com- manded by Burgevine, before this place." Gordon was no prisoner, however, but steadily operating for the reduction of Soochow ; the siege train was safe ; and the rebels were never more to approach Shanghai.

On Sept. 29, he took Patachow, close up to the southern verge of the Soochow suburbs, and wrote home next day that he expected in two or three mails to announce the fall of the

great city. An illustration of the curious condition of this strange war is afforded in the
circumstance that a bridge at Patachow formed
a sort of neutral ground where Gordon's European officers (European must in this connection
be held to include American) were in the habit
of having friendly intercourse with the people
of their own colour who were in the rebel army.
They were old comrades in many instances,
although they were now serving on opposite
sides. The rebel Europeans, as they may be
styled, were far from satisfied with their position
or their prospects. Gordon, for his part, was
willing to negotiate with them, because their
desertion would weaken the rebels, and place in
safety their own lives, which were now in
danger, for the rebel Wangs mistrusted them.
He accepted the proposal to give Burgevine
himself a meeting, and hear what that person
had to say.

A noteworthy man in his way, this Burgevine,
in sketching whose strange life a page may not
be thought wasted. A native of North Carolina,
his father had been one of Napoleon's officers.
He was a scholar and had been a gentleman,
who made shipwreck of his life, because of

ambition unsupported by steadfast purpose, of restlessness, and finally drink. Dr. Wilson says of him, "A much wandering man, he seems to have turned up in California, Australia, the Sandwich Islands, India—where he studied Hindustanee,—Jeddah, London, and other places; being in fact one of those nautical gentlemen who combine a taste for literature with the power of navigating coasting vessels, and, would fate allow, of founding great empires." He tired equally of a post-office clerkship and of editing an American paper, and so naturally gravitated to China, which was at that time to the adventurers of the world what Central America had been in Walker's day, and Germany during the long fighting of the Thirty Years War. We have already found him Ward's lieutenant and temporary successor, and his dismissal from the charge of the Ever Victorious Army has been recorded in a previous page. He never ceased to resent this dismissal; but continued to nourish his revenge against the Imperialists and his dream of carving out an empire in China; and it was in pursuit of both aspirations that he entertained the Tai-ping overtures, and as we have seen, took a detachment of miscellaneous foreigners to Soochow, and identified himself with the Tai-ping cause. The Tai-pings wished to have him, no doubt for the double reason that he and the Europeans he brought would make them more formidable in the field ; and in the belief too, that he had sufficient influence with the officerhood of Gordon's force, to bring them over, and perhaps the force itself along with them. He had become dissatisfied with his position in Soochow, and it was therefore that he entered into personal communication with Gordon.

At his interview Burgevine avowed his determination to desert the Tai-pings, if his officers and men were guaranteed immunity for acts done in the Tai-ping service. Gordon gave this guarantee, offering further to take a number of them into his own force, and assist the remainder out of the country. At a second interview, not understanding Gordon's character, Burgevine made him the proposal that they two should unite to seize Soochow, hold it equally against Rebels and Imperialists ; organise there an army of 20,000 men, and then march on Pekin. One can fancy the quiet scorn with which Gordon "declined to entertain any such idea." It was rather a ticklish time for Gordon, since, aware of the negotiation with Burgevine, the Imperialists ventured to suspect his loyalty ; while, on the other hand, he was running the risk of his own officers being tampered with. But in October the coup came off. Burgevine and his comrades sent word that they intended, under pretence of making a sally, to throw themselves on Gordon's protection. He gave the pre-arranged signal ; the Europeans headed what looked like a desperate rush on the " Hyson," backed by thousands of Tai-ping troops. The Europeans boarded the little vessel, the Tai-pings were driven off with volleys from her artillery, and she carried the fugitive deserters into Gordon's camp. But when they were landed it was found that Burgevine and several others were not among them. They accounted for this by stating, that being under suspicion, they took the opportunity when it offered, without waiting for those who were not at hand. They were glad enough to get out of their plight, poor wretches ! They had been virtually crimped from Shanghai by Burgevine, and had been badly treated in Soochow—starvation and death staring them in the face. Most of them volunteered to join Gordon's force.

Gordon at once made an appeal to the Taiping chiefs on behalf of Burgevine and his companions who still remained in Soochow, aware that he and they had been arrested. With his own hand he wrote a letter of admirable tone. Having referred to his own clemency and his endeavours to deter the Imperialist authorities from inhumanity, he continues, "Having stated the above, I now ask your Excellencies to consider the case of the Europeans in your service. A man made to fight against his will is not only a bad soldier, but he is a positive danger, causing anxiety to his leaders, and absorbing a large force to prevent his defection. If there are many Europeans left in Soochow, I would ask your Excellencies if it does not seem much better to you to let these men quietly leave your service if they wish it; you would thereby get rid of a continual source of suspicion, gain the sympathy of the whole of the foreign nations, and feel that your difficulties are all from without. Your Excellencies may think that decapitation would soon settle the matter, but you would then be guilty of a crime which will bear its fruits sooner or later. In this force of mine, officers and men come and go at pleasure, and although it is inconvenient at times, I am never apprehensive of treason from within. The men have committed no crime, and what they have tried to do, viz., escape, is nothing more than any man, or even animal, will do when placed in a situation he does not like. . . . You need not fear them communicating information. I knew your force, men and guns, long ago, and therefore care not to get that information from them."

The Tai-ping general answered this letter in very polite terms; and Burgevine was sent out safely from Soochow, and handed over to the American Consul. In a home letter Gordon mentions: " Moh-Wang asked the messenger (who brought him Gordon's letter) a great deal about me, and if it were possible to buy me over, and was told that it was not. He asked why the Europeans wanted to run away, and was told it was because they saw there was no chance of success. He said, ' Do you think Gordon will take the city?' and was told ' Yes '—which seemed to make him reflect. This defection of the Europeans is an almost extinguishing blow to the rebels, and from the tone of Moh-Wang's letter, so different from the one he wrote General Staveley a little time ago, I feel convinced that the rebel chiefs would come to terms if they had fair ones offered. I mean to do my best to bring this about; and am sure that if I do, I shall gain a greater victory than any captures of cities would be. . . . I care nothing for a high name."

Subsequent investigation proved that at the very time Burgevine was negotiating with Gordon in regard to his relief, he had proposed to his lieutenant a plan for entrapping the man whose efforts were being directed toward the succour of him and his followers. Jones revolted against treachery so base, and he and Burgevine had a "difficulty." Jones told the story thus : " Burgevine drew out his revolver, which he cocked and discharged at my head from a distance of about nine inches. The bullet entered my cheek and passed upward; it has not yet been extracted. I exclaimed, ' You have shot your best friend !' His answer was, 'I know I have, and I wish to God I had

killed you!'" There is a fine cynical frankness in the comment on this statement which
Burgevine sent to a Shanghai paper—"Captain Jones' account of the affair is substantially
correct; and I feel great pleasure in bearing
testimony to his veracity and candour, whenever
any affair with which he is personally acquainted
is concerned."

Burgevine subsequently had a strangely
chequered career, which cannot here be followed. When a prisoner in the summer of
1865 in the Imperialist hands, he was reported
to have been drowned by the capsizing of a
ferry-boat. "I have no reason to suppose,"
writes Dr. Wilson, "that the account of his
death given by the Chinese authorities was
untrue; and if they did drown him purposely,
they saved themselves and the American authorities a good deal of trouble."

By dint of hard, although desultory fighting,
now attacking, now defending, and hampered
by the clumsy and independent manœuvring of
Ching at the head of the Imperialist army in
so-called co-operation, Gordon had made good
the occupation of a chain of posts encircling the
east and the south sides of Soochow, close up

to Lake Taiho. There remained, to complete
the investment, but the reduction and occupation of the Tai-ping outworks on the north and
north-west of the city; then the chain of en-
vironing posts would extend from the lake
round to the lake, on whose waters his armed
steamers would in effect shut in the place and
its garrison. The character of the enterprise
had considerable analogy to the German siege
of Paris, only that Gordon had no "field-army"
such as those with which Prince Frederick
Charles, Manteuffel, and Göben covered the
Teuton cordon that encircled the capital of
France. Gordon had to neutralise numbers
by skilful dispositions and bold strokes to a far
greater extent than was incumbent on the German leaders. Including the contingent under
Ching which co-operated with him, and was
under his orders to a certain indefinite extent,
he had fourteen thousand men, all told, at his
disposal, for the double task of hemming in a
force more than twice his own numbers, and of
keeping off and hindering from relieving the
place other forces nearly threefold his strength.
The Tai-pings inside Soochow may have la-
boured under discouragement, for they had

learned to know Gordon; but at Wusieh, the Chateaudun of Soochow, there stood a fresh army 40,000 strong; which the Faithful King had marched down from Nanking, bent on unclasping Gordon's grasp on Soochow. That army, however, was to some extent paralysed by the critical situation of the Heavenly King's capital; Gordon had learnt how matters stood with Nanking, and so made bold to ignore the propinquity of the Faithful King and his 40,000 men.

He had left his Imperialist allies holding the southern posts, and had swept round to the north of Soochow with his siege-train and the lively Hyson for the reduction of the Tai-ping positions in that quarter. On November 1st he carried Leeku by assault, with the loss of an officer, who fell by his side leading the forlorn hope, and whom he had shortly before pardoned for something suspiciously like treachery. Eleven days later he went at Wantí, a place whose capture would all but complete the investment. It was so strongly built that shell-fire had no effect on it, so he carried it by storm, with some loss, but 350 rebels fell and 600 were made prisoners. He had men fighting under him at

G 2

Wanti who had been in the rebel ranks a week previously. There remained to be reduced only Mouding, on the Grand Canal; and this effected, the investment of Soochow was complete.

Returning to the eastern face, he determined to assail the defences of Soochow by a night attack, which was delivered November 27th. He himself commanded his forlorn hope of two companies, having Majors Williams and Howard under him. The mass of his force waited under arms for a signal to advance. The surprise seemed complete. The forlorn hope had penetrated through the outer works, and the main body was following, when suddenly a fierce fire of grape and musketry was opened on the whole force. Artillery replied to artillery, and Gordon, at the head of his forlorn hope, dashed at the breastwork. But there was hesitation behind him; his Chinese soldiers did not relish night-fighting, and Gordon had to fall back with considerable loss of officers as well as of men. Moh-Wang, the Tai-ping general, was himself in the forefront of the defence, fighting like a private soldier, with twenty Europeans around him. He repelled the attack, but his loss must have been very heavy from Gordon's artillery, which maintained its fire for three hours.

Now ensued some curious work. General Ching had an interview with one of the Tai-ping Wangs, who stated the general conviction inside the city that notwithstanding Gordon's temporary repulse, its reduction was simply a question of time. All his colleagues, with the exception of the indomitable Moh-Wang, who had a handful of junior officers supporting him, were prepared to yield the place, and come over to the Imperialists with the whole garrison. But to save appearances, Gordon must make another assault. While Moh-Wang was resisting that, the other Wangs would shut him out of the city, and so, free from his opposition, they would agree on a surrender. On the morning of the 29th, Gordon's artillery reopened on the stockades. The assault followed. It was arduous work. Ditches had to be swam across, breastworks had to be climbed, and the Faithful King him-self, who had arrived from Wusieh the same morning by a path still open, was engaged in the defence at the head of his body-guard. In the confusion of the attack Gordon, with a few men, found the Tai-pings in force between him and his supports.   To fall back was impossible as distasteful ; he fought his way onwards instead.   Capturing some stockades, he pushed through them, and had gained a stone fort when his troops overtook him, and made good the advantage he had won.   The position he had achieved rendered Soochow untenable by the Tai-pings ; but it had cost him dear.   Nine of his officers had been killed, and a great number wounded, among the latter his adjutant-general Major Kirkman.   As ever, Gordon had in those assaults exposed himself with a cool matter-of-fact daring that seemed natural to the man, and was necessary as an example to his motley force, but which would have been a vice in the commander of a more regular army. He never carried any other weapon than a little cane, with which he used to direct his followers, and which got for itself the name of " Gordon's magic wand of victory."   His Chinese soldiers, seeing him always in front among the bullets, yet never wounded, concluded that he bore a charmed life, and that it was the " magic wand " which gave him protection.

Some negotiations speedily followed, but the surrender was not just yet.   Stout old Moh-

Wang was still in the way. He called a council of war. It must have been a strange scene, when dinner over, and prayers offered up, the Wangs arrayed in their robes and crowns took their places around the raised table at the head of which sat the valiant Moh-Wang. The debate grew warm. Kong Wang rose from his throne and cleared for action by taking off his robes. Moh-Wang demanded to know what he meant; whereupon the other, probably the quicker of the two "on the draw," stabbed Moh-Wang with a dagger, and the other Wangs finished him off.

The same night Soochow surrendered. Gordon withdrew his forces to a distance, to prevent looting, and demanded a grant of pay for his men, as reward, compensation, and encouragement. Governor Li haggled with him like a fishwife, and Gordon had a difficulty in hindering his troops from revenging themselves directly on that official. He sent them back to Quinsan out of harm's way, but in a condition of disaffection approaching mutiny.

Li was intoxicated with the success which Gordon had earned but for which scant credit was accorded him. It is certain that the Tai-ping Wangs surrendered, but it is not clear to whom—whether it was to Gordon, to Ching, or to Governor Li, they considered themselves as capitulating. Anyhow Gordon had the fullest right to expect that Li would spare the lives of the Wangs. For mercy to them Gordon had expressly stipulated, and Li had "gladly assented" to the demand. Li never attempted to deny this, which was confirmed to the fullest extent by General Ching.

But Li betrayed his pledge to Gordon, and was guilty of an act as ruthless as it was treacherous —for he had accorded terms to the Wangs; an act that sent a thrill of indignation through civilisation, and ultimately withdrew British officers from service under the Imperial Government. It is a lurid story, the details of which Gordon has tried to write dispassionately. On the afternoon of the 5th of November, the day before the actual consummation of the surrender, General Ching set Gordon's mind at rest by telling him that Governor Li had "amnestied the prisoners." Next day, returning from marching his troops out to Quinsan, Gordon rode into the city to the Nar-Wang's house. There he found all the Wangs, their horses saddled, just starting to go out to Governor Li, for the meeting at which the city would be formally given over. In his anxiety to be assured that everything was well, he called aside the Nar-Wang, who told him all was right. Then he bade the Wangs good-bye, and saw them ride away toward the East Gate, bound for their rendezvous with Governor Li.

Gordon himself then took things easy, for his mind was at rest. He saw burial given to Moh-Wang's body, and then sauntered to the East Gate. Beyond it, tied up to the bank, lay Governor Li's boat. On the bank, close to it, he noticed a large crowd, and presently a horde of Imperialist soldiers came yelling in through the East Gate, firing off their muskets after their fashion. Gordon rebuked the rioters for conduct calculated to create a disturbance. Then General Ching came through the gate. When he saw Gordon confusion fell upon him. Ching lamely parried Gordon's questions with prevarications. The Wangs, he said, had never been to Li. Gordon returned that he had seen them going, and asked what could have happened to them. Then Ching told a cock-and-bull story which Gordon mistrusted. He betook himself for information to Nar-

Wang's house, which he found gutted, for the plundering had begun. Nar-Wang's uncle, himself a Tai-ping leader, begged that Gordon would go to his house for the protection of his womenfolk, and Gordon complied. He was now in effect a prisoner, for the Tai-ping soldiers, with arms in their hands, crowded the street outside. But he took no thought for himself. He boded mischief to the Wangs at the hands of Li, whose breach of faith he suspected. He did not then know that they had been murdered before he had the colloquy with Ching, and that the crowd of Imperialists he had seen on the bank near Li's boat had been standing around their corpses. Fortunately for him the Tai-pings were in equal ignorance of the fate that had befallen their leaders. A prompt and resolute man, Gordon decided on a masterful expedient to save the Wangs from the fate he did not know had already befallen them. He attempted to send out his interpreter to the trusty skipper Davidson, with orders to bring the steamers round and take prisoner the Chinese Governor-General; also to have his force brought up from Quinsan. He had difficulty in procuring permission for the interpreter to go out, but at length the latter was allowed to go at 2 A.M. on the 7th. An hour later, news came back that the Imperialist plunderers had seized the interpreter, wounded him, and torn up the order of which he was the bearer. The Tai-pings were becoming more and more excited, while the Imperialists were carrying on the work of plunder, and Gordon became apprehensive of a general massacre. Then he persuaded the men who held him virtual prisoner to let him go. He made an effort to reach his steamers, but was for an hour a prisoner in the hands of the Imperialists at the South Gate, who did not know him, and took him for one of the rebel Europeans. Escaping, he headed then for the East Gate, where he knew his body-guard was lying. Unrelenting in his resolve to seize Governor Li, he waited there for his steamers, and meanwhile kept his promise to the Tai-pings who had released him by sending his guard to protect the house of Nar-Wang's uncle. It was too late, however, and the house had been ransacked. General Ching turned up; Gordon gave him a piece of his mind, and remained waiting for the steamers to come up for his intended capture of Li, ignorant still that the Wangs had been be-headed. As he waited, Ching sent to him Major Bailey, an Imperialist artillery officer, with intent to speak him fair. Ching, said Bailey, after Gordon had spoken so sternly to him had " gone into the city, and sat down and cried." Then he had got up, and to relieve his sorrow, " shot down twenty of his men for looting," and sent Bailey to explain that he, Ching, had simply obeyed Li's orders. Gordon asked Bailey if the Wangs had been beheaded. Bailey replied, equivocatingly, that he had heard so. He then brought up Nar-wang's son. The lad pointed across the canal, and said that his father and the other Wangs lay dead there.

Gordon crossed over. " I found six bodies," he wrote, " and recognised Nar-Wang's head. The hands and bodies were gashed in a frightful way, and cut down the middle."

It is said that he burst into tears at the sight. They were tears not alone of sorrow, but of disappointment, shame, and fierce wrath. The foulest despite had been done him. His honour had been mocked at by the wanton butchery. " It is not to be wondered at," writes Mr. Hake, " that Gordon was enraged beyond bounds; it

is not surprising that for the first time during
the war he armed himself and went out to seek
the life of an enemy. He took a revolver and
sought the Governor's quarters, fully resolved
to do justice on his body and accept the
consequences."

But Li had come to realise what manner of
man Gordon in his wrath could be, and had
escaped into the town. Gordon pursued him,
but the Governor got into hiding, and remained
there. Gordon had ordered up his troops to
assist him in his search, but, finding that vain,
led them back to Quinsan. There he told his
officers that no British officer could serve longer
under Governor Li; that he did not intend to
disband the force, but would place it under
General Brown, the British commander at
Shanghai, and let him dispose of it.

Till near the end of February, 1864, Gordon
held the Ever Victorious Army inactive in
its quarters at Quinsan, under formal instructions from General Brown to suspend all active
aid to the Imperialist cause, further than pro-
tecting Soochow. These instructions were dic-
tated at Gordon's instance, and it was also on
his demand that an inquiry was instituted at

Pekin into the conduct of Governor Li. Meanwhile Li's despatches had described to the Imperial Government the success achieved in the reduction of Soochow. Li had of course arrogated to himself the lion's share of the credit, and was rewarded with the "Yellow Jacket," which carries with it the highest military grade of the Empire. But he had allowed himself to testify to the high value of Gordon's services ; and the Imperial Government was neither slow nor chary in its acknowledgments. An Imperial Decree set forth that "Gordon, in command of his auxiliary force, displayed thorough strategy and skill, and has put forth most distinguished exertions." It ordained, further, that "a medal of distinction of the highest class" be conferred upon him, and that he should receive a gift of 10,000 taels (about £3,500), in token of Imperial approbation. Li was enjoined to communicate to Gordon "our decree of approval and praise for the great bravery and exertions which attended the recapture of Soochow," and to present him with the money gift; and the instructions proceeded: "Foreign nations already possess orders of merit under the name of 'Stars.' Let, therefore, the decoration of the first class, which we have conferred upon Gordon, be arranged in accordance with this system."

Gordon was in no mood to be the grateful recipient of Imperial favours. He was scarcely the sort of man to be chagrined that Governor Li had stolen his laurels. Neither laurels nor honours were things about which Gordon concerned himself. "As for the honours," he wrote home, "I do not value them at all, and never did." But his indignation had not cooled at the despite done to him in the violation of the stipulation he had exacted that the Tai-ping chiefs should be spared. He would accept neither decoration nor money. It was in these terms he couched his curt refusal: "Major Gordon receives the approbation of His Majesty the Emperor with every gratification, but regrets most sincerely that, owing to the circumstance which occurred since the capture of Soochow, he is unable to receive any mark of His Majesty the Emperor's recognition, and therefore respectfully begs His Majesty to receive his thanks for his intended kindness, and to allow him to decline the same."

The Chinese Government in a financial sense

had behaved fairly well to the Ever Victorious Army, since £7,000 had been distributed to the wounded in the attacks on Soochow, and the extra month's pay that Gordon had agreed for had been paid. But inaction was deteriorating that force ; and yet more the prospect of his resignation of the command. "The officers," wrote one of them, "did everything to honour Colonel Gordon, and show in how high esteem they held him ; but they were very jealous of each other, and during January constantly quarrelled over the question who should succeed to the command in the event of his leaving." Sixteen of them had to be discharged. The urgency became great that Gordon, having put his hand to the plough, with so great effect, should not look back until the last furrow of the field had been turned. And if the good work was to be finished, it was clear that only he could accomplish it. During his inaction the rebellion, in spite of the fall of Soochow, began to make head again. The province was lapsing into lawlessness. Foreigners were joining the Taiping ranks. The irrepressible Burgevine was meditating a return to a service of which his experience had been so adverse. The Im-

perialist forces, despite the aid of some of
Gordon's disciplined artillery, were barely
holding their own against the enemy. Mr.
Robert Hart, the able and clear-headed official
in charge of the Imperial Customs, strongly
urged that Gordon should resume the field,
since his inaction was the strongest encourage·
ment to the disaffected, and pointed out that
his abandonment of that attitude could be as-
cribed only to his sacrifice of private feelings
for the welfare of the province in whose behalf
he had already done so much. Governor Li, for
his part, had something to urge in explanation,
or rather indeed in justification of the executions
he had ordered. Gordon so far stifled his re-
sentment as to have a personal interview with
the Governor, who agreed to issue a proclamation clearly setting out that the massacre was in
the teeth of the pre-arrangement with Gordon
that lives should be spared. Gordon intimated
to the British Minister in Pekin his resolution
to re-take the field. The language he used
proves how ready he was to accept responsibility when he had convinced himself that his
course was right. " I am aware," he writes,
" that I am open to very grave censure for the

H

course I am about to pursue ; but in the absence of advice . . . , I have made up my mind to run the risk. If I followed my own desire, I should leave now, as I have escaped unscathed, and been wonderfully successful. I do not apprehend that the rebellion will last six months longer if I take the field. It may last six years if I leave. . . . If the course I am about to pursue meets your approbation, I shall be glad to hear ; but, if not, shall expect to be well rebuked. This letter will relieve you from any responsibility on the matter."
The course he was about to pursue did meet Sir Frederick Bruce's approval, and that Minister further strengthened Gordon's hands by obtaining a positive promise in writing from the Chinese Government that, in cases of capitulations where he should be present, nothing was to be done without his concurrence. Accordingly, on the 19th of February, Gordon moved out from Quinsan with his whole force, save a garrison of 200 men left in that place under Colonel Morant. It was in the dead of winter, and the weather was bitterly cold and snowy,

In his letter to Sir F. Bruce, Gordon had

succinctly set forth his strategic scheme,—"I propose to cut through the heart of the rebellion, and divide it into two parts by the capture of Yesing and Liyang." Soochow, whence in effect he started, is in the very centre of the Kiangnan peninsula, to the western side of which the Tai-pings had been mainly localised by the previous fighting. At the north-west corner of the peninsula is Nanking, where the Heavenly King, the head of the rebellion, had his residence. On a waved line between Soochow and Nanking, were the towns of Yesing, Liyang, and Kintang, in succession from Soochow; all three strongly held by Tai-ping forces. By marching on this wavy line, and the successive reduction of the towns named, Gordon would cut the rebellion into two slices, each so circumscribed as probably to be unable to exist independently. This bold strategy had difficulties in its train. Shanghai could no longer be Gordon's base of supplies; he had to relinquish a base and march *omnibus impedimentis.* Nor could his steamers uniformly accompany him, and their support had therefore occasionally to be sacrificed. His troops were not what they had been. The recruited Tai-pings that now mainly filled the ranks were sturdy fellows enough, and did not lack courage; but they had not had time to acquire the discipline and steadiness which were the elements in virtue of which, next to the genius of its chief, the Ever Victorious Army under Gordon's leadership had hitherto justified its title. He had lost many of his best officers, some in fight, others by dismissal or withdrawal; and some of their successors were the reverse of efficient.

He moved by the north of Soochow to Wusieh near the Grand Canal, and thence marched on Yesing, through the region which the Tai-pings had been wasting during three years of uninterrupted occupation—a region which had been almost denuded of inhabitants, the few remaining being in the last stage of starvation. Yesing was captured after a petty resistance on March 1st, and a village occupied which cut the communications with Liyang, the next Tai-ping city in the line of route. In this village were found starving wretches who had been forced to resort to cannibalism. "Those who still remained alive had been driven to eat human flesh, and the unburied bodies of the dead were in a condition which showed that much of this revolting food had been consumed." Liyang was reached on the 4th, and so out of heart were the rebels there, that they surrendered without a blow. A thousand of its garrison were enlisted into the Ever Victorious Army and formed into a separate regiment : and twenty-five gun-boats captured were added to Gordon's flotilla. The country around it was in a ghastly condition. One of Gordon's officers writes : "Hundreds of dead bodies were strewn along the roads—people who had died from starvation ; and the few who were yet alive watched one of their comrades dying, so as to obtain some food off his dead body ! " The town was well stocked with provisions, all of which that Gordon could spare from his own necessities he distributed among the miserable peasantry. Leaving part of his force in Liyang, he marched forward on Kintang with three regiments of infantry and a strong artillery carried on the gun-boats. Bad weather and the necessities of the peasants had detained him, and it was not till March 20th that he was within striking distance of the latter strong place, whose garrison had not complied with a summons to surrender. Next

day everything was ready for opening fire, when
there reached him an alarming despatch from
Governor Li. Gordon had been trusting to the
Imperialists to cover his flanks, but they had
failed him. A Tai-ping army, 7000 strong, had
moved out from Chanchufu, a town north-west
from Soochow, and now almost directly in his
rear; had turned the Imperialist flank, was
threatening Wusieh, had captured Fushan, and
was besieging Chanzu, the town whose relief
had been Gordon's earliest enterprise with the
Ever Victorious Army, and so was within thirty
miles of Quinsan itself. This was startling
news, but Gordon had in hand the specific business of the reduction of Kintang. He would
concentrate himself vehemently on that, and so
free himself to deal with the other matter. .

. But Kintang proved stubborn. Three hours'
bombardment had made a practicable breach.
The rebels seemed cowed, and an assault was
ordered. Then they manned the breach, and
resisted with persistent determination. The renewal of the artillery fire swept the breach clear,
and a second storming party, led by Major Kirkman, attacked again, only to be also repulsed.
Kirkman was struck down wounded; and now

the magic spell of Gordon's immunity from hostile bullets was to be broken. He shared in the assault, and was shot through the leg. He silenced a soldier who was proclaiming the disaster, and stood giving orders till he all but fainted from loss of blood. Even then he would not retire, and Dr. Moffit had to carry him to his boat by main force. A third assault was attempted, but unsuccessfully; and Gordon had to draw off, with a loss of 100 killed and wounded, among whom were fifteen officers, two of whom were killed. He abandoned further attempt on Kintang, and on the 24th had reconcentrated at Liyang.

There yet more ominous tidings reached him from the Imperialists; the Faithful King himself was in possession of Fushan. Gordon's wound prevented him from standing, but, like Marshal Saxe, he could fight on his back. And time pressed. The advancing Tai-pings were issuing proclamations, that their march was on Shanghai, taking Soochow on the way. Even at Chanchufu they had been nearer Soochow than was Gordon at Liyang; how much more so when they were actually threatening Wusieh, not ten miles to the north-west of Soochow! It behoved him urgently, above all things, to recover the command of the interior lines.

The troops he had taken up to Kintang were worn by marching and fighting. He would not spare himself, wounded though he was, but the soldiers were not inspired by his perfervid energy. He had to take with him troops that had not been on the Kintang march; there were available but the light artillery and two infantry regiments, one of which consisted of the Tai-pings mustered in at Liyang in the beginning of the month. With this little force, little over 1,000 strong, he started for Wusieh on the 24th. Arriving there next day, he found that the Tai-ping force threatening it had been driven back, but that from Changchufu to Fushan, the whole northern region of the peninsula was in Tai-ping hands. Next day, with his artillery and 400 infantrymen, he dashed out into the territory which the Tai-pings pervaded, bent on discovering their dispositions, and the point at which they could be struck to greatest purpose. There was real sublimity in the serene confidence of this wounded man, lying prostrate and helpless on the deck of his boat, but plunging with a few hundred men into the heart of a region occupied by unknown thousands of enemies. In the district passed through the houses had been burnt, and the inhabitants butchered in every direction. The halt for the night was by a group of blazing villages, whence at dark the Tai-pings had been driven; and it was disturbed by a desultory fire on the sentries, alternated by efforts on the enemy's part to ride through the bivouac of the little force. It was through awful scenes that he darted with his amazing rapidity. A letter says : " It is horrible to relate ; it is more horrible to witness. To read that people are eating human flesh is one thing ; it is another to see the bodies from which the flesh has been cut. No one can eat a meal here without loathing. The poor wretches have a selfish look that is indescribable, and they haunt one's boat in shoals, in the hope of getting some scraps of food. Their lamentations and moans completely take away any appetite which the horrors one has witnessed may have left one. The rebels have evidently swept up everything edible, and left the unfortunate inhabitants to die."

Advancing, and fighting as he advanced, Gordon soon realized the situation. Waisso

was the centre of the Tai-ping line, on which
the rebels stood, with their backs to the
Yangtsze and their faces towards Quinsan,
By striking at Waisso, he would curl in that
left flank of theirs that stretched to Chanzu
and threatened a fresh country. Waisso,
then, became his objective.

He had to wait a day or two for his other
infantry battalion to come up, and then he
moved on the place. When a leader
essays a bold emprise and succeeds, the brilliancy of his tactics is praised, for nothing
succeeds like success; when he fails, he is stig-
matized as rash. Gordon has a profound in-
difference to criticism; but he is a man of
rigorous inward searching, and I think it possible that when he reviewed this Waisso business in cool blood, he may have realized that
he had been somewhat over-adventurous. By
dividing his force, he had often conquered.
But it was a very small force he had now, and
its elements were not wholly satisfactory. One
regiment of it was the best corps in the
Ever Victorious Army, but the other consisted of the Liyang Tai-pings, and had not
had time to acquire discipline. It is noteworthy

that in the majority of his divided movements he had remained with the infantry, and fought that arm himself. This he would probably have done at Waisso, but for the helplessness of his wounded condition. The officers to whom he intrusted the infantry operations proved unequal to the duty.

Gordon himself, with his artillery flotilla, pushed on up a creek that would take him close to the enemy's position. His infantry had orders to march the following morning, their direction was given them, and the combined attack was to be made the following day. Everything miscarried. The infantry had not come up to co-operate, and in their default the flotilla narrowly escaped destruction. The banks of the creek were too high to admit of their being swept by the guns, and the Tai-pings in force fired down into the boats. It was with great difficulty that the gun-boats were extricated, and a retreat made on the encampment. There the wildest confusion prevailed, and a panic was in full sway. The infantry had come by a great mischance. The force had advanced in the morning till it had come upon a Tai-ping camp, strongly entrenched and stockaded. Colonel Rhode, who was in command, probably felt the want of artillery. He might have remedied that by an immediate and resolute attack. Instead, he and Colonel Howard—the two regiments were marching apart—halted, and set about distributing their force in companies. The Tai-pings, from the adjacent hills, saw their opportunity. They worked in between Rhode and Howard ; then they came on in great numbers, and brought cavalry to the attack. The new regiment broke, stampeded into the other, and threw it into confusion. A regular rout ensued, and lasted for three miles up to the camp at Lukachow, where the pursuit was checked by the camp reserve. About 400 men were lost, and eight officers fell either in the fight or in the flight. It was an Isandlwana on a small scale in almost every detail, but that the slaughter was not so sweeping : few of the Tai-pings had other weapons than knives and spears. Gordon had no other alternative but to fall back, and hearten his men after the punishment they had received. He brought up another regiment, and, on 3rd April, reapproached Waisso, and effected a junction with Governor Li at the head of 7000 Imperialist troops.

The rebellion in the field had been driven to its last ditch; Nanking, its headquarter, was to hold out a little longer. In the limited area they still held up in the north of the Kiangnan peninsula, the Tai-pings were hemmed in on three sides by Imperialist troops, and on the Yantsze behind them was the Imperial fleet. In the infliction of the *coup de grace* Gordon's force had an important share. He first cleared the rebels out of Waisso with very little fighting. Then he followed them up as they retreated westward in disorder on Chanchufu and Tayan. The villagers rose against them in a fury of well-earned hate, and slaughtered them in thousands. Governor Li was besieging Chanchufu, and Gordon having collected his whole force, about 3,000 strong, moved to co-operate in this work. In the course of the preliminary operations he lost his best artillery officer, Major Tapp, and at the same time had himself a very narrow escape. It was arranged that on April 27th, after a preparatory bombardment, Gordon's troops and an Imperialist force should make a simultaneous assault at separate points. At 1 p.m. Gordon's attack was launched; two regiments formed the storming

party. The resistance was exceptionally desperate, and spite of the gallant exertions of the
officers, the column had to be recalled. The
combination had not come off; the Imperialist
attack had been delayed; so the whole Tai-
ping force had been free to oppose Gordon's
storming party. Later in the afternoon, both
forces, however, attacked simultaneously. The
Tai-pings fought with extraordinary desperation;
as they manned the breach Gordon's artillery
swept them down, only to be replaced again
and again by indomitable defenders, brandishing spears and shouting defiance. A retreat
had to be ordered, and even the pontoons had
to be abandoned. Gordon's loss in officers
was terrible; he had ten killed, and nineteen
wounded.

Then Gordon set the Imperialists to sap up
to the walls, and meanwhile the gradual defection of the garrison set in. A final assault was
made by Governor Li on 11th May, the anni-
versary of the capture of Chanchu by the Faithful King. The Ever Victorious Army had been
rather left out of the programme for this day.
The Imperialists duly attacked, but when they
crossed the ramparts, met with a desperate

resistance, and began to give way in confusion. At this critical moment Gordon struck in opportunely with a portion of his force. The Imperialists were rallied, the breach was cleared, and after some stubborn fighting inside the place the reduction of Chanchufu was completed. Its garrison was found to consist of 20,000 men, of whom 1,500 were killed at the capture. At that capture the Ever Victorious Army fought its last fight.

The Imperialists did not want it at Nanking, and outside the walls of that place the rebellion was crushed, and all but dead. The .Ever Victorious Army had done its work and "served its time." Its *raison d'être* was finished. Before the fall of Chanchu-fu Gordon had written home, " I shall, of course, make myself quite sure that the rebels are quieted before I break up the force, as otherwise I should incur great responsibility, but on these subjects I act for myself and judge for myself ; this I have found to be the best way of getting on. I shall not leave things in a mess, but I think, if I am spared, I shall be home by Christmas." He about kept his tryst.

When Gordon marched his army back into

Quinsan on 16th May, he learned that the Order
in Council had been cancelled under which British
officers were free to serve the Chinese Government. He saw many arguments in favour of
the immediate dissolution of the Ever Victorious Army; and he promptly set about the
work of disbandment. This, his last duty in
China, he handled with the same firm yet deli-
cate touch that had brought him through so
many difficulties, and with the characteristic disinterestedness which commanded respect alike
from the force, his countrymen, and the Chinese
officials. Governor Li gave him full powers,
and left in his hands the whole details. The
pay throughout had been good, and there was
no parsimony at the end. The officers who
had been wounded received about £900 apiece,
and the others in proportion. The unarmed
rank and file had a month's pay and marching
money to their homes. The disbandment had
been completed by the 1st of June. "And so,"
writes Chesney, "parted the Ever Victorious
Army from its General, and its brief but useful
existence came to an end. During sixteen
months' campaigning under his guidance, it had
taken four cities and a dozen minor strong

places, fought innumerable combats, put *hors de combat* numbers of the enemy, moderately estimated at fifteen times its own, and finding the rebellion vigorous and aggressive, had left it at its last gasp, confined to the ruined capital of the usurper."

The large money present offered to Gordon he declined, as he had done the previous grant. He had spent his pay in promoting the efficiency of his force. " I leave China as poor as when I entered it," were the simple, modest words he wrote home. He left China, however, with the goodwill, respect, and esteem of all with whom he had to do. The merchants and bankers of Shanghai expressed their collective gratitude. The British Minister wrote, " Lieutenant-Colonel Gordon well deserves her Majesty's favour, for independently of the skill and courage he has shown, his disinterestedness has elevated our national character in the eyes of the Chinese." The Emperor of China conferred on him the highest military title of China (Ti Tu, Commander-in-Chief) and the rare Imperial decorations of the Yellow Jacket and the Peacock's Feather.

Prince Kung formally requested the British

I

Minister to bring Colonel Gordon's merits before the notice of her Majesty, and adds: " Colonel Gordon's title, Ti Tu, gives him the highest rank in the Chinese army; but the Prince trusts that if, on his return home, it be possible for the British Government to bestow promotion or reward on Colonel Gordon, the British Minister will bring the matter forward, that all may know that his achievements and his character are equally deserving of praise."

It may be possible to bring many accusations against the system of government which obtains in these Islands; but it cannot be charged that Britain does not know how to reward her distinguished men. Prince Kung's aspiration had been anticipated. Already in the beginning of 1864, Gordon had received the exceptional distinction of a brevet Lieutenant-Colonelcy. But further recognition awaited him on his return to England. The guerdon usually bestowed on British subjects who have covered themselves with glory on foreign service in which other troops were engaged than our regular army, is the G. M. G., and even the most sanguine of Gordon's friends could scarcely have anticipated for him a higher distinction than this. But it was evident that there was a special delight to do him honour. He was made a C. B. And to mark further how his merits were appreciated, the defence of the kernel of the Empire was confided to his charge. This was the real nature of the work which Colonel Chesney permits himself to designate as " the building of obscure forts from the designs of others on an Essex swamp."

CHAPTER III.

GRAVESEND AND THE EQUATOR.

FROM 1865 to 1871 Gordon lived at Gravesend, employed on the duty of improving the defences of the Thames. These were his six years of quiet peace and beneficent happiness. It is a beautiful life of which Mr. Hake gives us a sketch so tender. "He lived wholly for others," writes that gentleman. "His house was school and hospital and almshouse in turn, was more like the abode of a missionary than of a commanding officer of Engineers. The troubles of all interested him alike. The poor, the sick, the unfortunate, were ever welcome, and never did supplicant knock vainly at his door. He always took a great delight in children, but especially in boys employed on the river or the sea. Many he rescued from the gutter, cleansed them and clothed them, and kept them for weeks in his house. For their benefit he established reading classes, over which he himself presided, reading to and teaching the lads with as much ardour as if he were leading them to victory. He called them his 'kings,' and for many of them he got berths on board ship. One day a friend asked him why there were so many pins stuck into the map of the world all over his mantelpiece; he was told that they marked and followed the course of the boys on their voyages; that they were moved from point to point as his youngsters advanced, and that he prayed for them as they went, night and day. The light in which he was held by those lads was shown by inscriptions in chalk on the fences. A favourite legend was 'God bless the Kernel!' So full did his classes at length become that the house would no longer hold them, and they had to be given up. Then it was that he attended and taught at the Ragged Schools, and it was a pleasant thing to watch the attention with which his wild scholars listened to his words."

The workhouse and the infirmary, writes another, were his constant haunts, and of pensioners he had a countless number. Many of the dying sent for him in preference to the clergy, and he was ever ready to visit them. All eating and drinking he was indifferent to : his philosophy was that in half an hour after a meal it did not matter what he had eaten. His large garden was cultivated much on the allotment plan, by poor people to whom he gave permission to plant what they pleased, and to take the yield. He allowed the author of a book on the Tai-ping Rebellion to come and stay with him, and supplied him with material. But there came to him a suspicion that the writer was praising him, and he asked to see what he had written. It was a bad quarter of an hour for the author, who ruefully told Gordon he had spoiled his book, as he watched page after page being torn out. His purse was always empty because of his free handedness ; and he even sent some of his medals to the melting pot in the cause of charity.

When another appointment removed him from Gravesend, there was universal regret. Equally graceful and sincere was the tribute of the local newspaper. " Our readers will regret," it wrote, " the departure of Colonel Gordon from the town in which he has resided for six years, gaining a name by the most exquisite charity that will long be remembered. Nor will he be less missed than remembered, for in the lowly walks of life, by the bestowal of gifts; by attendance and ministrations on the sick and dying; by the kindly giving of advice; by attendance at the Ragged School, Workhouse, and Infirmary; in fact by general and continual beneficence to the poor, he has been so unwearied in well doing that his departure will be felt by numbers as a personal calamity. His charity was essentially charity, and had its root in deep philanthropic feeling and goodness of heart; shunning the light of publicity, but coming even as the rain in the night time that in the morning is noted not, but only the flowers bloom and give a greater fragrance. . . All will wish him well in his new sphere, and we have less hesitation in penning these lines from the fact that laudatory notice will confer but little pleasure upon him who gave with the heart and cared not for commendation."

The "new sphere" was Galatz, the Roumanian river-port on the lower Danube, and his duty there, as British member of the Danubian Commission, was to superintend the improvement of the navigability of the great river's mouths. The deep Sulina channel by which vessels of large burden can now load at the Galatz and Braila wharfs is mainly Gordon's work during the two years his head-quarters were at Galatz. I found his memory still green there in the early days of the Russo-Turkish War, fourteen years after he had exchanged the mosquitoes of the lower Danube for the not less venomous insects of the Upper Nile. How that exchange came about was in this wise.

When Mehemet Ali entered on the enterprise of annexing the Soudan to Egypt, his honest intentions may have been to introduce commerce and civilisation into the midst of the Negro and Arab tribes, its inhabitants. Trading ports were established, but it was soon found that slave hunting paid better than ivory, and the traffic in slaves gradually increased until the scandal of it stirred the indignation of Europe. The Egyptian Government connived in the slave catching and the slave dealing, and made a profit out of what was a virtual royalty. The Upper Nile Basin—the region now known as the Equatorial Provinces—was the main theatre of the abominatiou. It was in this country that Zebehr—now known as Zebehr Pasha, and suggested by Gordon as the new Governor-General of the Soudan—rose to be the arch slave hunter, who was able to defy the Khedive, and even to defeat an expedition sent to humble his pretensions. At length the remonstrances of civilisation moved the late Khedive to evince, or feign, a serious earnestness of intention to put down the slave trade. He formally announced the annexation by Egypt of the whole Nile Basin up to the Equatorial Lakes, and in 1869 issued a firman to Sir Samuel Baker, giving him absolute and supreme power over the whole country south of Gondokoro. Sir Samuel had previously been up to the equatorial part of the Nile system, and must have been aware that the command assigned him was mostly on paper. Of his work there is no space to speak, but spite of the steadfast opposition he experienced, alike from Egyptian officials and their accomplices the Arab slave traders, he gave the cruel commerce a severe blow. Baker's term was up in 1873 ; and in 1872, Nubar Pasha and Gordon had met in Constantinople, and Nubar had asked the Danubian Commissioner to recommend some Engineer officer to be Baker's successor. A year later, when Baker was coming out into civilisation from his thankless and laborious work, Gordon tendered himself as his successor if the Khedive would apply for him and the British authorities did not object. The arrangement was effected, and after a short visit to London to make his simple preparations Gordon arrived in Cairo in February, 1874.

A quotation from Mr. Birkbeck Hill's abstract of the Khedive's Instructions which Gordon took with him to his province will best explain the character of the duties to which he was assigned in Central Africa. " The province which Colonel Gordon has undertaken to organise and to govern is but little known. Up to the last few years it had been in the hands of adventurers who had thought of nothing but their own lawless gains ; and who had traded in ivory and in slaves. They established factories and governed them with armed men. The neighbouring tribes were forced to traffic with them whether they liked it or not. The Egyptian Government in the hope of putting an end to this inhuman trade, had taken the factories into their own hands, paying the owners an indemnification. Some of these men had nevertheless been still allowed to carry on trade in the district, under a promise that they would not deal in slaves. They had been placed under the control of the Governor of the Soudan. His authority, however, had scarcely been able to make itself felt in these remote countries. The Khedive therefore had resolved to form them into a separate Government, and to claim as a monopoly of the State the whole of the trade with the outside world. There was no other way of putting an end to the slave trade which at present was carried on in defiance of law. Once the brigandage had been stamped out, trade might become free to all." Gordon was to establish a line of posts through his province, attempt to win the confidence of the tribes, and persuade them to stop the wars made in the hope of carrying off slaves.

Gordon's career in Africa is recorded in those supremely interesting and intensely character-istic letters to members of his family which Mr. Birkbeck Hill has had the privilege of publish-ing, and which really make his book—"Colonel Gordon in Central Africa." I own to shudder ing at the sacrilege of condensing into a few score pages the outlines of that extraordinary narrative which those letters—Gordon's own journal in effect—tell with so unstudied a vividness. That the path of the condenser is a thankless one—this does not distress me. My grief is that in "boiling down" this thick volume of letters, the beauty, the strength, the sacred fervour, and the tender play of humour which irradiate them must clean evaporate, and there be left but a matter-of-fact record of acts and facts. I have the self-consciousness of being a vandal; yet there comes to me some consolation in the probability that its very succinctness which distresses me will induce many people to read this little book who cannot find time to study the massive volume of letters, and so learn at least something more of this grand and beautiful life than they did before. To those wonderful letters there is now an added pathos. The field that Gordon broke in to cultivation threatens to relapse into pristine wilderness. The march of humanity that he led so enthusiastically halted when he withdrew from its van. And now it has wheeled in its tracks, and is in melancholy and disheartening retreat.

Before Gordon left Cairo on his way to his work, he had seen through the devices of Ismail. "I think," he wrote home, "I can see the true motive of the expedition, and believe it to be a sham to catch the attention of the English people; and feel like a Gordon who has been humbugged." But he was determined as far as in him lay to make the sham into a reality. "I will do it," was his later expressed resolution, "for I value my life but as naught, and should only leave much weariness for perfect peace." The Egyptian authorities wanted to make a satrap of him, and he was offered £10,000 to maintain his state; but Gordon named £2,000 and refused to accept any more. But an *entourage* was incumbent. He had to engage a suite of servants, of whom he was not long in ridding himself, and two wretched aides-de-camp were assigned him, much against his and their will. Going by water to Souakim, he travelled through the desert to Berber—a fortnight's march, for he had an infantry escort of 200 troops. Subsequently he traversed the distance, 280 miles, in nine days on camel-back. At Khartoum, the man who in the river voyage up from Berber, "had his trousers off and was pulling the boat in spite of crocodiles," was received by the Governor-General in full uniform, salutes were fired in his honour, and the braying of a brass band welcomed him. His own official title he diseovered to be " His Excellency General Colonel Gordon, the Governor-General of the Equator "—he calls it "an extraordinary mixture." He stayed but eight days in Khartoum, by no means favourably impressed with the Governor-General there, with whom he afterwards had many "skirmishes." His Equatorial policy he defined in a decree which he published before leaving Khartoum. " I have issued," he writes, "a stinging decree, declaring the Government monopoly of the ivory trade, and prohibiting the impórt of arms and powder, the levying of armed bands by private people, and the entry of any one without passports—in fact, I have put the districts under martial law."

Then, on 22nd March, he began his voyage up the Nile, accompanied by his *protégé* Abou Saoud, whom he had found a prisoner in Cairo. Abou's character was villainous, and everyone united in dissuading Gordon from taking with him the notorious slave hunter, but he was obstinate. He believed in Abou, and sanguine that he would be "a very great help—he will be a great man; he is built and made to govern." The disillusionment came when he discovered, later, that his life was in imminent danger through this scoundrel's treacherous machinations. There are buoyancy and hope in Gordon's narrative of this voyage; he was not yet in harness, and had not come into the realisation of the difficulties that were to confront him. He notes the crocodiles "lying glistening in the sun," the huge flocks of migratory birds "waiting to go north," the hippopotamuses "walking about like huge islands in the shallow water," the monkeys with their "tails stuck up straight over their backs like swords," the camelopards that "looked like steeples." He gets fun out of his surroundings. One night, he tells, a peal of laughter from a bush startled him. "I felt put out, but the irony came only from birds that laughed at us from the bushes in a very rude way. They are a species of stork, and seemed in capital spirits, and highly amused at anybody thinking of going up to Gondokoro with the hope of doing anything." At the Saubat River, he had his first interview with some of his subjects—a tribe of Dinkas. The chief was coaxed on board—"he was in full dress— a necklace," and his method of salutation was perhaps a little peculiar. "He came up to me, took up each hand, and gave a good soft lick on the backs of them; then he held my face, and made the motion of spitting on it." From the "tight place" in the Bahr Gazelle the "sudd," or vegetation that had blocked the river so that it took from eighteen months to two years to voyage from Khartoum to Gondo- koro, had been partly cut, partly swept away, and Gordon passed in a few hours the stretch that had lately been so obstructive. A few days below Gondokoro he passed first the abandoned Austrian Mission Station of St. Croix, where in thirteen years fifteen mission- aries had succumbed to local diseases without having made a single convert; and Bohr, a " regular slave-trading station, where they were not over civil when they heard of my decree." At length, twenty-three days out from Khar- toum, Gondokoro was reached, and Gordon's arrival created much amazement, for nobody had ever heard of his nomination.

Gondokoro was the nominal capital of his province, but the province itself was purely mythical. The only possessions Egypt held in all the vast region were two forts, one here at Gondokoro, with a garrison of 300 miserably inefficient men, whom it were a misnomer to call soldiers; and another at Fatiko, some 200 miles as the crow flies further to the south, with 200 men holding it. Both places were virtually in a state of siege. "As for tax-collecting," he . writes, " or any government existing outside the forts, it is all nonsense. You cannot go out in safety half a mile—all because they have been fighting the poor natives and taking their cattle." The man chiefly to blame for this state of things was Raouf Bey, the Egyptian Governor whom Gordon relieved. Raouf, he complains, " had never conciliated the natives, never had planted dhoora (grain), and, in fact, only possessed the ground he camped on." Very soon Gordon dispensed with the supine, inefficient Raouf, who was not sorry to get away—left, in fact, "in great joy and contentment."

It was at least a fine virgin field on which to begin work, and Gordon was quite sanguine. " I apprehend not the least difficulty in the work; the greatest will be to regain the poor

K

people's confidence. They have been hardly treated." But he could not commence in earnest until his staff and baggage had come up, and he made a dash down the Nile to Berber to fetch them. His sole companion hitherto had been the American Colonel Long, whom he left to represent him at Gondokoro. The staff he found at Berber consisted of Major Campbell, of the Egyptian Staff; Mr. Kemp, his engineer; the two brothers Linants; Messrs. Anson, Russell, and Gessi; and, later, there came to him Lieutenants Chippendall and Watson, R.E. The Berber journey cost him over two months, but in June he was back at the Saubat River, where he remained two months, organising a station there and conciliating the Shillook natives. Here he began to see his way into the heart of the slave commerce. There were three slave stations above him on the Bahr Gazelle, to the occupants of which he had given notice to quit. From one of them a letter came into his possession directed to the Egyptian Governor of Fashoda, a post on the Nile outside Gordon's confines. This letter ran: "I am on my way to you with the 2,000 cows I promised you and with *all* to satisfy your wants." The cows had been stolen from the neighbouring tribes—the *all* meant slaves. Gordon went straight to the slave station, broke it up, cleared the holders of it out, and ordered them down to Khartoum; the cows he had to confiscate, since the owners could not be reached. The convoy of another dealer he patiently waited for at the Saubat. The trader tried to pass his convoy round Gordon, but the latter "checkmated" him, gave him a fortnight's imprisonment and then forgave him, and even employed him. " He is not worse than the others, and these slavers have been much encouraged to do what they have done. He is a first-rate man, and does a great deal of work." " In reality," he continues, "it was not I who changed the station (to a better site across the river), but the slave-hunters whom I have taken into my employ. They are hardy, active fellows, mostly Berberans—the remnant of an ancient race." As he waited for a steamer to take him up to Gondoroko, he engaged himself in making friends with the natives around him, and in studying the character of the local slavery. His views expressed then may throw some light on the line he has taken in regard

K 2

to slavery since he reached Khartoum in January last. "I think," he writes, "that the slavers' wars, made for the purpose of taking slaves, are detestable; but if a father or mother of their own freewill, and with the will of the child, sells that child, I do not see the objection to it. It was and is the wholesale depopulation of districts which makes slavery such a curse, and the numbers killed or who perish in the collection of slaves." Wretched as were the people, their apathy stood for something like contentment. "I declare," writes Gordon, "I think there is more happiness among those miserable blacks, who have not a meal from day to day, than among our own middle classes. The blacks are glad of a little handful of maize, and live in the greatest discomfort. They have not a strip to cover them, but you do not see them grunting and groaning all day long, as you see scores and scores in England, with their wretched dinner-parties and attempts at gaiety, where all is hollow and miserable." He filled up his time in charitable ministrations. "I took an old bag-of-bones into my camp a month ago, and have been feeding her up; but yesterday she was quietly taken off, and now knows all things. She had her tobacco up to the last, and died quite quietly. What a change from her misery ! I suppose she filled her place in life as well as Queen Elizabeth." Wretched, lonely, unwholesome quarter as Saubat was, it was a good spot for intercepting the slave traffic. A boat would come down from Gondokoro. Its appearance would be perfectly innocent—the cargo wood and ivory, seemingly, nothing contraband. But a bird would whisper to the alert Gordon, and a rummage would be made. The wood pulled up, lo ! a number of woolly heads, the heads of slaves whom the slavers were trying to smuggle down the river. " The strategical position here is splendid," writes Gordon, triumphant at such a find. Then slaves and ivory would be alike confiscated; the former he kept, the latter went to swell the revenue.

In the beginning of September he went up to Gondokoro to encounter fresh toil and trouble. For one thing, staff and servants were alike ill, broken down by the dreadful climate, which on him alone made no impression. The place was an hospital. Poor young Anson had already died. Gessi had been down with fever, but was now recovering. Russell was ill—too ill to be moved, and Gordon had him in his own tent, wholly under his charge. Campbell, ill ; Linant very ill, could not be moved. De Witt, " an amateur," dead. All the servants, ill and down. " The sick were being medically attended by," writes Gordon, " one of the best doctors (me) I know of." And the same practitioner had also to do most of the nursing. All the accounts Gordon had to keep, every detail personally to see to. But Gondokoro was too unhealthy. He moved his quarters first sixteen miles up the river to Rageef, a great change for the better, with its higher ground and purer air. Linant, however, could not be moved, and died at Gondokoro.

To add to Gordon's troubles, he found that Abou Saoud, in whom he had believed, was a scoundrel and a traitor. He had been "squeezing" the chiefs whom Gordon was trying to conciliate, bullying the natives, and treating Gordon himself with insolent familiarity. He had inspired his men to mutiny. So Gordon broke the ex-slavedealer, in whom he had hoped to find an efficient lieutenant, and sent him down to Gondokoro with this letter as a flea in his ear :—"Abou! when I took you up at Cairo, there was not an Arab or a foreigner who would have thought of employing you, but I trusted to your protestations and did so. When I got to Gondokoro you were behaving properly, and I congratulated myself on your appointment to the high post I gave you. Soon, however, I came little by little to repent my action, and to find out that my fair treatment was thrown away. You deceived me. To come to more personal matters, you strangely forgot our relative positions; you have forced your way into my private apartment at all times, have disputed my orders in my presence, and treated all my other officers with arrogance, showing that you are an ambitious grasping man, and unworthy of the authority I gave you. If you do this under my eyes, and at the beginning of your work, what will you do when you are away from me? Now, hear my decision! Your appointment is cancelled, and you will return to Gondokoro and wait my orders. Remember, though I remove you from your office, you are still a government officer, subject to its laws, which I will not hesitate to put in force against you if I find you intriguing."

Three weeks later, on the entreaty of two of his staff, Gordon relented, and gave Abou Saoud another chance.   But that person was "not a bit changed—only more wary and sly than before." He recommenced his intrigues; and Gordon would stand him no longer.   "One wants some forgiveness oneself," he had written, when he pardoned the scheming traitor; "and it is not a dear article."   It came very near being a dear article to Gordon, however, for through Abou's machinations he had a narrow escape of his life; so the end came, and Abou Saoud—a failure and something worse—was sent down the river. Gordon, however, lived inside a sort of ring-fence of scoundrelism.   He presently discovered that his local chief officer at Gondokoro had connived at the passage of a convoy of slaves for the "consideration" of 360 dollars.   The convoy—1600 slaves—got arrested down at Fashoda, and the Gondokoro Mudir had a rather unhappy time.   But Gordon had not a free hand, and felt the falseness of his position. The Khedive was writing to him "quite harshly" to stop the slave trade.   The Khedive's officials were helping it on.   "I ask," writes Gordon, "if under these circumstances

his Highness would think me justified in hanging
the men I find in charge of slaves : I do not think
he would. I cannot help thinking the Khedive
finds out that he has made a mistake in appointing me, and that he would sooner have a quieter,
easy-going, salary-drawing man."

At the end of the year he abandoned the
Gondokoro site for his principal station, and
transferred the seat of government to Lado,
twelve miles down the river, on ground that
rose above the pestilential marshes. He had
lost from sickness eight members of the original
staff, of which only Kemp now remained with
him at headquarters. Kemp had been up at
Duffli at the head of the cataract, 134 miles
south of Gondokoro, trying to put together the
steamer that had been taken up in pieces, and
that was still intended to be used later for the
navigation of the Albert Nyanza ; but troubles
with the tribes, caused by the misconduct of
Kemp's escort, had necessitated the temporary
abandonment of the work. Colonel Long had
been doing good work before going sick down
to Khartoum. He had visited M'tesa, the
King of Uganda, and had met with a good reception. On his way down he had discovered and

used a water passage from Urandogani to Foweira, which gave Gordon great satisfaction, facilitating as it would his access to M'tesa's capital.

Lado he found much healthier than had been Gondokoro. He had invented a pill which had kept him in perfect health, and hard work hindered him from feeling dull, spite of his absolute loneliness. He had completed a map of the Nile from Rageef down to Khartoum, and had built his new station at Lado when the year closed. It was about this date that one of his staff thus summed up what Gordon had already accomplished:—" He has certainly done wonders since his stay in this country. When he arrived, only ten months ago, he found a few hundred soldiers in Gondokoro, who dare not go a hundred yards from that place, except when armed and in bands, on account of the hostile Baris. With these troops Gordon has garrisoned eight stations, Sambat, Ratachambe, Bohr, Lado, Rageef, Fatiko, Duffli, and Makrane. Baker's expedition cost the Egyptian Government nearly £1,200,000, while Gordon has already sent up sufficient money to Cairo to pay for all the expenses of his expedition, including not only the sums required for last year, but the amount estimated for the current one as well."

For 1875 Gordon had a great scheme, if only he could persuade the Khedive to fall in with it. His communications with Egypt *viâ* Khartoum were the reverse of satisfactory. The navigation of the river was beset with difficulties, and firewood for the steamers was beginning to get scarce. Gordon's proposal for a new base was that the Khedive should send a small expedition to Mombaz Bay on the Indian Ocean, 250 miles north of Zanzibar, where a station should be established, and whence a detachment should push inland toward M'tesa. The Mombaz Bay route would be shorter than that by Khartoum, and would much more effectually open up Central Africa. The Khedive entertained the proposal, and sent out what was known as the Juba River Expedition, under McKillop Pasha of the Egyptian navy, whom Colonel Long accompanied to command the intended inland expedition. Trouble arose. Interests clashed. The Zanzibar merchants became alarmed for their equatorial trade, and the Aden settlement grew nervous about its Soumali coast supplies.

Finally, at the instance of the British Government, the expedition had to be abandoned.

In February Gordon went down the river to
the "pestiferous Saubat." His programme was
to spend eight months in settling the stations on
that line; then go south to Fatiko, taking up
to Duffli the steamers he meant to have put
together there, and with which the lacustrine
water system was to be explored. But circumstances interfered with the execution of this
programme. From Foweira there had come
news to him that Kaba Rega, king of Unyoro,
had leagued himself with the old slave-hunting
gang, the original licensees of the Egyptian
Government, and was meditating an attack on
that station. He ordered down the slave
hunters, who were still nominally in the Khedivial service. Fifty of them came and were
sent off to Khartoum, bewailing Gordon's masterful confiscation of the slaves they had brought
down to Lado. As for Kaba Rega, Gordon
determined to drive him out of his kingdom,
and substitute Riongo, who had been Baker's
vakeel and was now Kaba Rega's rival and a
well affected man.

But first the Sheikh Bedden had to be dealt

with, for he had been contumacious, and his proximity to Rageef rendered him dangerous. The only method to bring this apparently truculent gentleman to terms was to surprise him and take his cattle from him. Some risk attended the expedition, for Gordon's Soudanese soldiers were as bad as bad could be, and a concentration which he had devised failed to come · off by reason of their heedlessness and pusillanimity. But in the end, without any effusion of blood or burning of villages, Bedden was punished by the loss of 2600 head of cattle, and soon after came in and made submission. Gordon was not stern with the old man; he gave him back twenty of his cows, and made him some presents—anxious thus to impress the tribes with a sense at once of his justice and generosity. Later it turned out that the cattle had not been Bedden's at all, but belonged to a friendly chief, to whom prompt restitution of them was made ! Bedden himself turned out to be but a poor creature after all. " To-day," wrote Gordon, " I rode to Bedden Islet to have a look at the channel, and observing some natives on a rock under a tree, I walked up to them. They did not move, and I sat down near

them. I asked, 'Are you Bedden's people?'
They pointed to an old man and said 'Bedden,'
and there was our friend himself. Poor old
man! he was partially blind. I tried to be civil
with him; gave him my whistle and some
tobacco, and told the people not to take his
cows. It was a sudden meeting to come across
him like that!"

The problem that confronted Gordon was
how to get the heavy portions of the steamers
intended for the lakes up above the cataracts
about Duffli, which, with the rapids below them,
interfered with the continuous navigation of the
river. He finally resolved, that since the route
lay through a region that would be almost in-
evitably hostile, the true method was to "go up
and place a station on the Nile, a day's march
above Rageef; then to bring all the *impedi-
menta* up there; then to make another station
a day's march further, and take the things up
there; and so on to the head of the Falls." But
then the further problem was before him, how
to feed the people in those successive stations?
It was yet, however, early in the year, and he
could not begin the operation until later in the
season, when he should have reconnoitred the

country, and when his steamers would have arrived from Khartoum. He started southward to select the position for his first station, taking with him forty Soudanese soldiers, fifty Niam-Niam recruits from the Makrata country whom he had enlisted, and a number of bearers carrying fifteen days' provisions for the little expedition. Kerri, on the Nile, thirty miles south of Rageef, was the limit of the march. When halted there, and he was in friendly intercourse with the natives, the alarm of an attack was given, which formed a pretext for his "unruly mob" of followers to plunder the huts. It was a ruse, and angered Gordon so that he thus breaks out in his letter :—" Cowardly, effeminate, lying brutes these Arabs and Soudanese ! without any good point about them that I have seen. It is degrading to call these leaders and these men officers and soldiers—I wish they had one neck, and that someone would squeeze it ! When not obliged, I keep as far away as I can from them, out of earshot of their voices. It is not the climate ; it is not the natives ; but it is the soldiery which is my horror." By dint of hard work, in the early days of June three nuggars—Nile barges—were towed up the

narrow rapid stream from Rageef to Kerri, and
100 soldiers followed to form the station there.
Gordon himself went down to Lado to await the
steamers from Khartoum, which were long'over-
due, and which were bringing the troops he
needed.   It is needless to say he found there
everything as it should not be.   The impossible
Governor he " bundled off" to Khartoum—his
"Botany Bay," along with a number of pampered
and spoilt old soldiers.   And he had to deal
with the women belonging to the soldiers.   The
latter had been wont to have wives in every
station, which made the stations masses of in-
defensible huts.   Gordon compelled the "vifes,"
as he called them, to accompany these men to the
new stations which he was forming.   And he
was justifiably proud of the fact that now he
had so pacificated the region that a couple of
soldiers could march safely where previously it
was necessary to send a band 100 strong.

At length, on the last day of July, a start was
made from Kerri. He had to "pray the nuggars
up as I used to do the troops when they
wavered in the breaches in China," but it was
heart-breaking work. The soldiers were miserable, 'feckless' creatures, and the current was

strong, the tackle was bad, and there were many rocks. Occasionally there was defeat all along the line. " It appears that yesterday" (Gordon is writing August 9th) "one of the nuggars, through the stupidity of the Reis, broke loose, and floating down got into the middle of the rapids in such a position that nobody could get at her. In my absence they sent down the felucca, and she got staved in on the rocks and sand. Next they sent down another nuggar, and she is now in the middle of the river hard and fast on the rock." This was a "sad catastrophe," but perseverance overcame it, and the point where was to be formed Moogie Station was reached a few days later.

Here he waited for the reinforcements he expected up from Lado on the arrival of the Khartoum steamer, and soon, then "the two hemispheres will meet." The natives were troublesome. It was not that they sent their magicians to curse Gordon—that did not matter. But they attacked the station next to the one he occupied, and fired arrows into the tents of his own little camp where he had but twenty men. Next day young Linant, the brother of the Linant who had died at Gondokoro, came down from

L

Makadi, forty miles up stream, with ropes and a detachment, and a number of natives to assist in hauling the nuggars. Linant had been to M'tesa, and met there in April Stanley the explorer. Gordon's young assistant had not long to live. There had been a skirmish in which the natives showed unaccustomed courage, and Linant, with Gordon's permission, took a detachment of thirty-six men with two officers and crossed the river to make reprisals, with intent to deter the natives from attacking the expected steamer. This was in the morning. At midday Gordon heard firing, and saw Linant's red shirt as he stood on a hill, not two miles distant from the station, apparently in no trouble. In the afternoon there was an alarm. A man was seen running down to the opposite shore. A boat fetched him across. "Where is your musket?" asked Gordon. "The natives have got it!" "Where are the rest?" "They are all killed!" "How?" "They had finished their ammunition." Gordon had but thirty men and they were useless—in a panic at the news. He moved down stream to the next station, which was fortified, experiencing immense difficulty on the voyage because of the swift tortuous current. But the natives allowed the movement undisturbed, save that one from an eminence hurled vituperation. "I made him recognize," grimly remarks Gordon, "that the top of a rock 500 yards distant was not a healthy place to select for the delivery of an address." He found at the lower station the steamer and four escaped men of Linant's party, who told the story that the detachment had got surrounded, and that when all its ammunition was gone the natives had rushed in. Poor Linant was killed by two lance wounds, a victim of the bright red shirt he wore—the second son his father had lost in the Equatorial Province.

It was necessary to punish this reverse, and Gordon had received a great accession of force. The steamer had brought up a detachment, and the Mudir of Fatiko, Nuehr Aga, who turned out an excellent officer, brought in a number of fierce and strapping Niam Niams, so that the Moogie garrison was now 500 strong. But Gordon could not find it in his heart to be very relentless against those hapless natives, whose wizard "stood on 'Balak's hill,' obeying, no doubt, the Chief's mandate, 'Come, curse me this people, for they are too mighty for me'—the Kings and Princes of Midian sitting like

L 2

apes behind him." "I can quite enter," writes Gordon, "into these poor people's misery at their impotency. 'We do not want beads; we do not want to see the Pasha; we want our lands, and you to go away!'" The retributive expedition killed nobody, and brought in but 200 cows, 1,500 sheep, and the daughter of the Sheikh, who, of course, had to be let go.

At length Duffli was reached. "IT IS ALL OVER," writes Gordon in large capitals. The Fola Falls were impassable, and everything would have to be *portaged.* He settled down at Fashelie, a few miles from Duffli, to wait until the tall grass would burn that now waved around him like a great sea. He was ailing. He suffered from ague for the first time since boyhood, and later came liver. The rest helped him, and gave time for administrative work. The chain of stations from the Soudan up to almost within touch of the Albert Nyanza, was complete. The posts arrived regularly; the country was actually almost at peace. And the slave-hunting? He had been industriously routing out the slave-catchers, but up at Duffli he found "a little nest of ten," who had stayed behind in hopes that they would be overlooked.

No such luck for them! They had been quite independent, levying taxes and making raids; but their good time was over very soon after Gordon reached the scene of their perform- ances. Probably they did not feel very ami- able towards him when they found themselves inexorably "bundled off" down to Khartoum, they and their gang of followers.

By the end of 1876 Gordon had finished his Equatorial work and was back in London, but when that year opened he had still perhaps the most arduous part of his undertaking before him. The region of the Great Lakes had to be explored in detail, pacificated, and studded with posts to maintain the peacefulness. The early days of January saw him marching south from Fashelie to Foweira *viâ* Fatiko, through a dreary country strewn with outcrops of iron ore and with slag from native smelting. The region between Duffli and Foweira was a lonely desert of marsh, out of which "the moment the sun goes down, a cold damp arises, that enters one's very bones." The thorns tore his clothes to rags, and gigantic elephants cumbered the diffi- cult track through the tangled jungle. His object in going thus far south now, was to chase

Kaba Rega out of his Unyoro kingship at
Mrooli, and restore Riongo. In this he succeeded ; Kaba Rega burning his " palace," and
running off to Masindi with the " magic stool."
Gordon left garrisons in Masindi and Mrooli to.
keep Kaba Rega in check and support Riongo,
and returned in February to Duffli, postponing
his intention for the present, of " surveying the.
gaps in the Victoria Nile." In the beginning
of March the two life-boats having been put
together at Duffli, Gessi started with them to
explore Lake Albert Nyanza. Reaching Magungo, where the Victoria Nile flows into Lake
Albert, Gessi set forth on his work of cir-
cumnavigation, which he accomplished in nine
days, in spite of a very violent storm that drove
him on to an isle swarming with Kaba Rega's
troops, on whom it was necessary to fire. The
Lake Gessi reckoned 140 miles long by 50 wide.
Gessi earned Gordon's commendation ; he had
done his work smartly and efficiently, and rejoined his chief in the end of April. Meanwhile
Gordon himself was continuing his attention to
administrative details. He reconstituted the
line of stations from Duffli north to Lado, and re-
organised a postal service. From Foweira there

came down to him in an envelope addressed to "Stanley," a quaint letter from M'tesa, written in Kaba Rega's interest. The scribe was evidently a Bombay man, of a phonetic temperament. The letter is a curiosity.

"To Sir Canell Gorlden, Feb. 6, 1876. My dear Friend Gorden hear this my word be not angry with Kavarega Sultan of Unyoro. I have head that you been brought two manwar ships but I pray you fight not with those wanyoro for they know not what is good and what is bad. I am Mtesa King of Uganda for if you fight with governour you fight with the King. . . I pray you my friends hear this my letter stop for a moment if you want to fight put ships in the river Nile take west and north and I will take east and south and let us put Wanyoro in to the middle but first send me answer from this letter, Because I want to be afreind of the English. I am Mtesa son of Suna King of Uganda let god be with your majesty even you all Amen. Mtesa King of Uganda."

The humour of his lonely situation up in this remote region, left to struggle single-handed with every petty detail, rather amused than irritated the energetically philosophical man.

Steamers were wanted. The engines originally ordered out by Baker, then casually found by a travelling engineer half embedded in the desert sand beyond Korosko, had finally in a casual kind of fashion reached Khartoum. But the engines were useless without hulls. " Shall I order hulls and risk it ?" writes Gordon in a home letter. " Ask Mary what I had better do, or the old cook. . . In any other Government in the world I should have under me subordinates to look after the proper supplies being sent up and properly distributed, to look after the accounts, the soldiers, their arms, &c. I have not time to do this work, and it appears not to be the custom—the whole of these matters are the affair of the Governor personally. He is controller in land and water matters in the fullest extent of the word ; repairs of boats, steamers, &c., are all his work."

As Gordon moved through the country he used his observant faculties keenly. " It is odd and worthy of study," he writes—"the limits of perfect nudeness and of full clothing. The tribes on the Nile to the Albert Lake are perfectly nude ; then comes a region of apologies for dress, and then come full dressed tribes.

This is another curious feature about the Nile tribes : they have not the least idea of indelicacy in being naked, but they are very clean in person and in their habits and demeanour."

It was a tedious period while the completion of the steamer at Duffli was being waited for ; but at length it was ready. Gessi, the efficient, had been ordered down to Khartoum, and Gordon was unaccompanied in this latest expedition by any European. He had resolved not to undertake exploration work, and had indeed in the beginning of the year written to Sir Henry Rawlinson, pointing out that his troops in the stations which he had formed in the Lake Country needed all his efforts to keep them supplied. "The wants of the troops," he then wrote, "are immediate; the exploration can wait." But these gaps in the Nile geography were preying on his mind. "I see at once," he wrote, "how incomplete the work is until they are filled up." Schweinfurth had written, "It may be that Lake Albert belongs to the Nile system ; but it is not a settled fact, for there are seventy miles between Foweira and Lake Albert never explored, and one is not authorised in making the Nile leave Lake

Albert. The question is very doubtful." Gordon had followed the Nile from Khartoum to
Duffli, and Gessi had completed the survey of
the river from Duffli up into Lake Albert. An
" Albert Nile" then was established ; but what
about the Victoria Nile ? That river flowed
out of the Lake Victoria Nyanza, and its course
was known as far north as Foweira ; but beyond
that, what of it ? There were those who held
it might go to the Saubat or the Asua, both of
which rivers are part of the Nile system, but in
this case the Albert Nyanza would be a separate
source.

"It was contended," wrote Gordon later,
" that the Nile did not flow out of Lake
Victoria and thence into Lake Albert and so
northward, but that one river flowed out of
Lake Victoria and another out of Lake Albert ;
and that these two rivers united and formed
the Nile. This statement could not be positively denied, inasmuch as no one had actually
gone along the river from Foweira to Magungo. So I went along it with much suffering,
and settled the question. I also found that
from Foweira to Karuma Falls there was a
series of rapids to Murchison Falls, thus by

degrees getting rid of the 1000 feet difference
of level between Foweira and Magungo."

On July 28, Gordon was on Lake Albert,
and had reached the debouchment of the
Victoria Nile into that lake. Then he began
his arduous survey work of the seventy miles
stretching eastward to Foweira. "A dead
mournful place this is" (near Murchison Falls),
"with a heavy damp dew penetrating everywhere; it is as if the Angel Azrael had spread
his wings over this land. You can have little
idea of the silence and solitude." The river
was navigable up to the foot of the Falls, but
then the arduous tramp began in a pouring
rain through dense jungle, and terrific ravines
coming down laterally from the table land into
the deep canyon in which the river ran. Five
days of scrambling through a tangle of wild
vines and other creepers at the rate of about
eighteen miles a day, brought Gordon to the
deserted station of Anfina, and three days later
he was in Foweira, and the survey had been
complete. He visited the station that had
been formed at Mrooli, seventy-five miles up
the Victoria Nile from Foweira, and penetrated
by land eighty miles further in the direction of

Lake Victoria, to near Speke's Nyamyango.
Then he turned back, and visited Masindi Station, thence arriving at Magungo on September
29th, having annexed for the Khedive and
actually occupied a large tract of the Equatorial
lucustrine region.   On 6th October he started
on his journey northward, bound for Cairo, his
ulterior intentions seemingly not very definite.
" Body of Comfort—a very strong gentleman—
says, 'You are well; you have done enough;
go home—go home and be quiet, and risk no
more.'   Mr. Reason says, 'What is the use of
opening more country for such a Government?
There is more now under their power than they
will ever manage.   Retire now, and avoid
troubles with M'tesa and the Mission.'   But
Mr. Somebody (I do not know what) says,
' Shut your eyes to what may happen in future;
leave that to God, and do what you think will
open the country thoroughly to both Lakes.
Do this not for the Khedive, or for his Government, but do it blindly and in faith.'   An oracle
also says, ' Let your decision rest on the way
the Khedive is disposed; if he desires you to
stay, then stay; but if he seems indifferent,
then do not hesitate, but go away for good.' "

Gordon reached Cairo on December 2, had a final interview with Cherif Pasha, to whom he entrusted the task of informing the Khedive that he did not intend continuing in his service, and on Christmas Eve, 1876, he arrived in London. He had administered the Equatorial Province for eighteen months. What he had done in that time was briefly this :—He had mapped the White Nile from Khartoum to within a short distance of the Victoria Nyanza. He had given to the slave trade on the White Nile a deadly blow. He had restored confidence and peace among the tribes of the Nile Valley, so that they now freely brought into the stations their beef, corn, and ivory for sale. He had opened up the water communication between Gondokoro and the Lakes. He had established satisfactory relations with King M'tesa. He had formed Government districts, and established secure posts with safe communication between them. He had contributed a revenue to the Khedivial exchequer, and this without oppression. The Tai-ping Rebellion established Gordon's genius as a military commander; the Equatorial Provinces, when he left them, testified not less to his genius as a philanthropic and practical administrator.

CHAPTER IV

GOVERNOR-GENERAL OF THE SOUDAN.

"THEY say I do not trust Englishmen!" once said shrewd old Ismail. "Do I mistrust Gordon Pasha? That is an honest man; an administrator, not a diplomatist." For the moment Ismail had lost his "administrator." Gordon had suffered so much hindrance in his Equatorial work at the hands of Ismail Yacoub Pasha, the Governor-General of the Soudan, that he had thrown up his command. He had successfully checked slave-driving in his own Province, but he could do nothing to stop it in the extensive Soudan region, where Khartoum was the head-quarters of the system. But the Khedive was urgent for him to return, and it was pointed out to him by those in authority at home that there was a sort of moral obligation resting on him to carry out his work. His holiday in England was brief; he was back in

Cairo early in February, 1877. He conquered all along the line. Ismail Yacoub was removed, and his place given to Gordon, with a vastly increased sphere of duty and responsibility. "Setting a just value," wrote the Khedive to the latter on February 17, 1877, "on your honourable character, on your zeal, and on the great services you have already done me, I have resolved to bring the Soudan, Darfour, and the provinces of the Equator, into one vast province, and place it under you as Governor-General." He was to have three sub-governors, and the two matters to which Ismail desired his principal attention were the suppression of slavery, and the improvement of the means of communication.

Part of his commission was to attempt an arrangement of questions in dispute between Egypt and Abyssinia, and this matter Gordon resolved to go into before proceeding to Khartoum and beginning his work of administration. He had his interview with the Khedive. "He looked at me reproachfully, and my conscience smote me. . . . Then I began and told him all; and then he gave me the Soudan, and I leave on Saturday. I am very glad to get

away, for I am very weary. I go up alone
with an infinite Almighty God to direct and
guide me, and am glad to so trust him as to
fear nothing and to feel sure of success." He
was at Massowah already on the 26th of
February.

It was a tangled skein, the unravelment of
which was thrown upon Gordon by the Khedive's curiously vague instruction : " Il y a sur
la frontière d'Abyssinie des disputes ; je vous
charge de les arranger." Lord Napier of Mag-
dala's friend, Prince Kassai, had set himself up
under the title of " Johannis, King of Abyssinia." Old Menelek of Shoa, on the south,
still held and holds his own against Johannis,
and Bogos also remained recalcitrant. The ill-
fated Munziger Pasha, a Swiss, who was Governor of Massowah for the Khedive, had persuaded his master to snatch the opportunity to
annex Bogos to the Soudan. That was effected
in 1874, but when the lust for annexation
prompted a further effort to wrest the Hamaçen province from Abyssinia, the Egyptian
troops were utterly and disastrously defeated,
chiefly by the exertions of Walad el Michael,
the hereditary Prince of Hamaçen and Bogos,

whom Johannis had released from the confine-
ment in which he had been detained, and sent
him into his own country to raise his people
against the Egyptian invaders. Smarting under
defeat, the Khedive, in 1876, instituted a new
expedition against Abyssinia under the Ame-
-rican Loring and Rahib Pasha. Walad el
Michael had quarrelled with Johannis, and,
thinking he could do better for himself by
changing sides, went over to the Egyptians.
He brought them no luck. Johannis smote
them hip and thigh, and finally, under a truce,
what was left of the Egyptian army got back to
Massowah. · Walad el Michael, who had 7,000
men, drew off to Bogos; and while Johannis
and Rahib were negotiating, he struck for his
own hand, and surged into the Province of
Hamaçem, whose Abyssinian Governor he
killed. Johannis panted to have this truculent
free-lance in his power, and sent a mission to
Cairo offering the Khedive the cession of
Hamaçem—Bogos already he had—if the
Egyptians would but hand over to him this
troublesome Walad el Michael. The envoy
was treated in rather *haut en bas* fashion, and,
after kicking his heels in Cairo for some three

M

months, returned to Abyssinia without any answer from the Khedive to Johannis's proposal—an indignity which kindled the latter potentate to bitter wrath.

It was to attempt the resolution of this chaos into order that Gordon went up to the Abyssinian frontier. He could devote but a brief interval to the effort, for the internal condition of his new and vast Province clamoured for his urgent attention. Darfour was in revolt, and the Egyptian garrisons were besieged by the insurgents. Further south the slave-dealers, under the lead of that "cub" Suleiman, the son of Sebehr Pasha, were threatening an outbreak. And to crown the difficulties of the situation for Gordon, the Soudan had been well-nigh drained of troops for the support of the Sultan in his war with Russia. It availed Gordon little that the Khedive had made him a Marshal; sent him a uniform covered with gold lace, and given him in charge the South-eastern Littoral down to Berberah, opposite Aden. From Massowah he pushed on Keren (now Sanheit), the chief town of Bogos. His new state this man, so fond of simplicity, found "irksome beyond measure." He breaks out in

.angry protest : " Eight or ten men to help me
off my camel! as if I were an invalid. If I
walk, every one gets off and walks ; so, furious,
I get on again." As he approached Keren, the
Abyssinian mercenaries in Egyptian pay came
out to meet him with musicians, dancers, and
kettle drummers; when he entered, the garrison
was on parade to receive him. It was not the
inevitable Scot he found here, but the almost
equally inevitable Irishman, a gentleman of the
name of Macilvrey, who had come up with
Consul Cameron, and now wore his white
sheet, and had a local wife and family. Walad
el Michael presently came into the place with
an escort of cavalry and infantry. The French
missionaries interpreted to him Gordon's views.
Egypt declined to prosecute the war with Abyssinia, and Gordon would either give Walad a
government in his territory, or ask Johannis to
give him one in Abyssinia. Walad wanted
ever so much better terms, but Gordon was
resolute, and Walad accepted the former alternative. It was a complicated situation, which
Gordon thus expounds in quaint allegory :

"There were two courses open to me with
respect to this Abyssinian question ; the one to

M 2

negotiate peace with Johannis and ignore Walad el Michael, and if afterwards Walad turned rusty, to arrange with Johannis to come in and catch him. This certainly would have been easiest for me. Johannis would have been delighted, and we would be rid of Walad; but it would first of all be very poor encouragement to any future *secessions*, and would debase Egyptian repute. The process of turning in the polecat Johannis to work out the weasel (Walad) would play havoc with the farmyard (the country) in which the operation was carried on; and it might be that the polecat Johannis having caught the weasel Walad, might choose to turn on the hens (which we are), and killing us, stay in the farmyard. For, to tell the truth, we, the hens, stole the farmyard, this country, from the polecats when they were fighting among themselves, and before they knew we were hens. The other course open to me was to give Walad a government separated from Johannis, which I have done, and I think that was the best course; it was no doubt the most honest course, and though in consequence we are like a fat nut between the nutcrackers, it will, I hope, turn out well."

The "hen" simile Gordon pursued in a written reverie on administration. "I often think how small the office work generally is with us in England in our great offices, in comparison with the questions one has tó decide here. In the one case a few pounds are in dispute; in the other case the whole tenure, and the destinies of human beings are a question. In reality both are equally important so far as the effect on ourselves is concerned. The procuring and boiling of potatoes is as much to a poor woman as the reorganisation of the army is to Cardwell. We are all hens, and never were such eggs laid as our own!"

He could not wait here at Keren while slow thinkers made up their minds. His presence was needed at Khartoum, for which he started in the beginning of April, riding some forty-five miles a day on his swift camel; and giving orders, writing letters, and attending to applications at the stations which he passed through. The work he saw in front of him would be arduous; but he braced himself to wrestle with it. "With terrific exertions," he wrote, "I may in two or three years' time, with God's administration, make a good province, with a good army

and a fair revenue, and peace and an increased
trade, and also have suppressed slave raids ;
and then I will come home and go to bed, and
never get up again till noon every day, and
never walk more than a mile."

Arrived at Khartoum, he had to submit to
the ceremony of installation. The Cadi read
the firman and presented an address, a royal
salute was fired, and then Gordon had to
make his speech from the vice-throne. It was
very short—but "it pleased the people much."
The pithy sentence he uttered was, "With the
help of God I will hold the balance level ; " and
then, as not he records, he "directed gratui-
ties to be distributed to the deserving poor, and
in three days he gave away upwards of a thousand pounds of his own money." He was not,
however, universally popular. His second in
command, Halid Pasha, "wanted to bully"
him ; however, "after a two days' tussle" he
gave in and became Gordon's "dear friend and
obedient servant," but he had later to be dis-
graced and sent down to Cairo. The sister of
the late Governor-General took a petulant
method of signifying her disgust at her brother's
supercession. She broke all the windows of

the palace—some hundred and thirty—and cut
the divans to pieces out of spite.

Gordon spent less than a month in his capital,
but in that time he revolutionised the administration. Under the old régime ten or fifteen
unfortunates were flogged daily ; he abolished
the reign of the courbash. In the bad old
days, nobody could approach the Governor
without bribing the underlings, and every office
was got by dint of backsheesh. The regular
pay of the places was poor—not often more
than £240 a year—yet great bribes were given
by the aspirants, to be recouped to the office-
holders by corruption and "squeezing" the
people. The officials had been wont to bring
those bribes to their superior, for venality per-
meated the whole of the Egyptian machinery of
government. When the backsheesh was brought
to Gordon, he felt the impossibility of reform-
ing at a bound immemorial usage, so he took
the money and put it in the treasury. To
facilitate the redress of grievances, he had a
box in the palace-door, a "lion's mouth" in
which suppliants put their complaints and
petitions, which received his immediate attention, and the device saved him the waste of

time that would have been involved in giving a hearing to every petitioner. Before he left he decided on giving the city a proper water supply, and so spare the citizens the labour of carrying water from a distance. And he had already commenced the task of disbanding the 6000 Turks and Bashi Bazouks who constituted the frontier guards, and who habitually allowed the slave-caravans to pass.

It was a mighty task which he confronted, this reform of the Soudan. "A stupendous task," writes Mr. Hake, "to give peace to a country quick with war; to suppress slavery among a people to whom the trade in human flesh was life and fortune; to make an army out of perhaps the worst material ever seen; to grow a flourishing trade and a fair revenue on the wildest anarchy in the world. The immensity of the undertaking; the infinity of details involved in a single step toward the end; the countless odds to be faced; the many pests, the deadly climate, the horrible vermin, the ghastly itch, the nightly and daily alternations of overpowering heat and bitter cold—to be endured and overcome; the environment of bestial savagery and ruthless fanaticism—all these combine to make the achievement unique in human history."

Urgently wanted in Darfour, he left Khartoum toward the end of April, and journeyed rapidly by Obeid to Fogia, whence a force had been sent two months previously to relieve the Darfour garrisons. "I expect," he wrote during this journey, "to ride 5,000 miles this year, if I am spared. I am quite alone, and like it. I have become what people call a great fatalist, yet I trust God will pull me through every difficulty. The solitary grandeur of the desert makes one feel how vain is the effort of man. This carries me through my troubles, and enables me to look upon death as a coming relief, when it is His will. I am now accustomed to the camel. It is a wonderful creature, and so comfortable, with its silent, cushion-like tread." His camel was an exceptionally swift animal; as Gordon approached Fogia, it left the escort far behind, and its rider "came flying into the station in marshal's uniform" before the troops there had time to get into order to receive him. While waiting at Omchanga for troops to come to him—"tag, rag, and bobtail troops" were all he expected—he felt himself

constrained to ask pardon of the people for
their oppression by the Bashi Bazouks. Enterprise clashed with enterprise. Fascher, the
capital of Darfour, had to be relieved. Haroun,
the surviving member of the Darfour Sultan's
family, was in revolt. At Shakka, further
south, were the hordes of Zebehr Pasha the
arch-slaver; his son Suleiman in command.
"Shakka," he writes, "is the Cave of Adul-
lam; all murderers, robbers, &c., assembled
there, and thence make raids upon the negro
tribes for slaves. They can put ten thousand
men into the field. Altogether it was as well I
came to the Soudan; another year would have
left little Soudan to come to, what with these
gentlemen, Darfour and Abyssinia!" On the
march to Toashia, Gordon's "tag, rag, and bob-
tail" had no meat for two days, and he found
there a garrison that had received no pay for three
years—a set of brigands, whom he sent back
into Kordofan to be disbanded. He took on to
Dara 500 "of all sorts, a very poor set," and
on the way was threatened by an attack from
thousands of determined blacks. "Very few
Englishmen," he wrote, "know what it is to be
with troops they have not a bit of confidence in.

I prayed heartily, but the situation gave me a pain in the heart. I do not fear death, but I fear, from want of faith, the results of my death —the whole country would have risen. It is most painful to be in such a condition; it takes a year's work out of one." At Dara there came to him with 600 men the Sheikh of the Razagat tribe, from near Shakka, smarting under outrage at the hands of Sebehr's son. Dara had been six months without news from without; everything was at famine prices. Gordon likens his arrival to the relief of Lucknow. Indeed the whole country was starving. Among some hundreds of wretched creatures believed to be slaves, captured outside Dara, there were "poor little wretches, only stomachs and heads, with antennæ for legs and arms—the enormous stomachs caused by grass feeding."

He was determined to deal with Shakka and with Suleiman, but first he had to push out to Fascher and ascertain how matters fared with the supine garrison of 8,000 men in their nominal beleaguerment. But he had to go round from Dara by Wadar, for the Leopard tribe was threatening Toashia. He had for ally the Masharin tribe, whose chief was mortally wounded in the first fight. Seven hundred "Leopards" attacked his camp, in which he had 3,500 troops, but so cowardly were they that the Leopards all but conquered, indeed would have done so but for the exertions of the brave Masharins. His plan of coercing the Leopards into submission was by driving them from their wells—a policy from which his humanity revolted, but it produced the desired effect. The Leopards made their submission ; their plight, "with throats unslaked, with thick lips baked," was piteous in the extreme. Gordon had compassion on them, swore them to fealty on the Koran, and then let them drink. The Leopards had got their lesson.

Gordon could afford to stop in Fascher only sufficiently long to banish a colonel who had been intriguing against him. Zebehr's son had to be dealt with. The "cub" had sent Gordon a temporising letter, but his acts did not accord with his words. News reached Gordon from the fugitives who had suffered, that the slave-dealing horde under Suleiman was ravaging the region about Dara and even threatening that place itself. He dashed at Dara, riding eighty-three miles in a day and a-half, and leaving his escort far behind. As soon as his people there had recovered from their surprise at his sudden arrival they proceeded to fire the salute that should have greeted him. "My poor escort," writes Gordon, "where is it? Imagine to yourself a single, dirty, red-faced man on a camel ornamented with flies, arriving in the divan all of a sudden!"

Three miles outside Dara a gang of slavers who were stirred to anarchy by the orders of the arch-slaver Zebehr, and who had just sworn on the Koran to persistent hostility against Gordon and the government he represented, several thousands of their slave-soldiers about them, and in command Zebehr's son himself. Inside Dara, a lone man, who had ridden in on his camel, and was speculating on the where-abouts of his escort. And what happened? Let the lone man tell the story himself. "At dawn I got up, and putting on the golden armour the Khedive gave me . . . rode out to the camp of the robbers three miles off. I was met by the son of Zebehr—a nice-looking lad of twenty-two years—and rode through the robber band. There were about 3,000 of them, men and boys. I rode to the tent in the camp;

the whole body of chiefs were dumfounded at
my coming among them. After a glass of
water, I told the son of Zebehr to come with
his family to my divan. They all came, and
sitting there in a circle, I gave them in choice
Arabic my ideas. That they meditated revolt;
that I knew it, and that now they should have
my ultimatum, viz., that I would disarm them
and break them up. They listened in silence,
and then went off to consider what I had said.
They have just now sent me a letter stating
their submission, and I thank God for it. . . .
Maduppa Bey has come here and says, when
the son of Zebehr got home, he lay down and
said not a word, and that the Arabs say I *have
poisoned* him with coffee." Gordon resolved to
send men to Shakka and clear out the "slave
nest." He ordered young Suleiman back there,
and, after a scene, the young fellow finally departed, leaving half his gang with Gordon. Before he went, Suleiman wrote subserviently to
ask Gordon for a government. The reply was
that until he had proved his fidelity Gordon
would never give him a place, even if the refusal
cost him his life. He was in the midst of men
who were debating whether or not they should

fight him, but this did not discompose him.
" Ruffians as they are," he writes, " I rather
like having a chat with them." The chat on
this occasion took a curious turn. When
Gordon had given his brusque reply to the
chief who brought him the letter from Suleiman, he asked the emissary whether he was a
father. " He said ' Yes,' and I asked him
whether he did not think a good flogging would,
do the cub good, to which he agreed."

Gordon followed Suleiman into the "den" at
Shakka, at the latter's invitation. There were
6,000 more slave dealers in the interior whom
he was determined to work out, and yet for
whom he felt some consideration. He had
been thinking out the slave question from the
slave-dealer's point of view, and was not quite
in accord with the home Abolitionists-at-any-
price. As to the slave-dealers he asks, "Would
you shoot them all ? Have they no rights ?
Are these not to be considered ? Had the
planters no rights ? I would have given
£500 to have had the Anti-Slavery Society in
Dara during the three days of doubt whether
the slave-dealers would fight or not. A bad
fort, a cowed garrison, not a man who did not

tremble,—a strong, determined set of men, accustomed to war, good shots, and with two field-pieces. Now understand me. If it suits me I will buy slaves for my army. I will let captured slaves go down to Egypt and not molest them, and I will do what I like and what God in His mercy may direct me to do about domestic slaves; but I will break the neck of slave raids even if it cost me my life. I will buy slaves for my army; for this purpose I will make soldiers against their will to enable me to prevent raids."

Suleiman behaved on the surface like a gentleman. He came out to meet Gordon, gave him a cordial welcome and the hospitality of his own house, which Gordon accepted. He seems rather to have taken to the lad, whom Gessi later had to exterminate. Suleiman's very coolness amused him. "He *is* a cub," writes Gordon. "He has no sense of propriety—lolls about, yawns, fondles his naked feet, and speaks as if he were a street boy. He quietly ignores all the past, and asked me for his back pay! He does not seem in the least put out at any hard words I may say. He would have suffered nicely if he had fallen into the hands of an Arab Pasha."

Shakka Gordon found swarming with slaves. When he left for Obeid, he could not help suspecting that the party travelling under his escort was actually a caravan of slaves. "When you have got the ink out of it that has soaked into blotting paper, then slavery will cease in these lands." His visit to Suleiman lasted only two days. Later he learned how narrow had been his escape from treachery.

He was back in Khartoum by the middle of October to find that his energy had made him "much feared and respected, but not overmuch liked." The whole population was impressed by his unquenchable force, his resolute firmness. "The Pasha is coming" was news that inspired alertness into every functionary. The mass of accumulated work at the capital he despatched in a week, and then set off by water down the Nile to Berber; with this mild programme: "Berber, Dongola, Wadi Halfa, Assuan; thence I cross to Berenice on the Red Sea, and go up to Massowah; from Massowah to Bogos; thence I hope to go to meet King Johannis; thence return to Massowah and go to Berberah and perhaps Harrar; then back to this place." Events disarranged the projected tour. When

N

below Dongola investigating a railway con-
tract, telegrams from Khartoum reached him,
announcing an invasion on the part of the
Abyssinians, and that Sennaar was actually
threatened. There was nothing for him but to
return with all speed to Khartoum, which he
did, making a " bee-line " across the so-called
Bayouda desert, to learn that the story of invasion was an invention. But the irrepressible Walad
el Michael was troubling the frontier, and Gordon rode off into the Bogos country to look up
that turbulent person. Walad he found at
Hellal, a mountain eyrie six hours from Sanheit, with 7,000 troops around him. Walad was
shamming sick ; Gordon found him lying on a
couch, nursing his knee. It was a hazardous
undertaking, accompanied as he was by but ten
soldiers. He was quartered in a wretched hut,
with a fence round it, and his people were con-
siderably scared at the aspect of affairs. While
waiting for the palaver with Walad, he amused
himself with an inspection of that leader's army,
and at night was serenaded by the priests with
hymn-singing. Walad would not hear Gordon's
suggestion that he should solicit pardon from
Johannis, and Gordon arranged matters with

him on the basis of a subsidy of £1,000 a
month, and left very willingly for Massowah,
whence, after waiting in vain some time for a
reply to a proposal he had sent to King Johannis,
he departed for Khartoum, viâ Souakim and
Berber. And so his first year of office closed.
During that year he had ridden over about 4,000
miles of desert, and had effected wonders of
reform. It had been dreadful labour. Continual
camel-riding had affected him curiously. " I
have shaken," he wrote, " my heart or lungs
out of their places ; and I have the same feeling in my chest as you have when you have a
crick in your neck. . . . I say sincerely that,
though I prefer to be here sooner than anywhere,
I would rather be dead than lead this life."

He did not reach Khartoum, intercepted at
Shendy by a telegram from the Khedive begging
him to leave the Soudan and come to Cairo
to arrange Ismail's and Egypt's complicated
finance. He was in Cairo by March 7th, and
on reaching the station at 9 P.M. was whisked
straight off, in all the dirt and dust of travel,
to dinner at the Palace, where the Khedive
placed him at table on his right hand. Quarters
were assigned him in the Kasrel Kousa, the

Cairo palace set apart for royal visitors—a splendour which he loathed. " My people are all dazed," he writes, " and so am I, and wish for my camel." In designing him for the "figure-head" of the Finance Inquiry, Ismail was mistaken in his man. Gordon was in too dead earnest for the work that was expected of him ; he spoke his mind with considerable emphasis, and he had left Cairo within a month after his arrival. He was not chagrined by what he calls his " failure," although he had the belief that, had he been permitted, he could have satisfactorily settled the finance trouble. Here is a sample of his philosophy :—" His Highness threw me over completely at the last moment ; but far from being angry, I was very glad, for it relieved me of a great deal of trouble ; and he said I might go at the end of next week. I laugh at all this farce. I left Cairo with no honours, by the ordinary train, paying my fare. The sun, which rose with such splendour, set in the deepest obscurity. His Highness was bored with me after my failure, and could not bear the sight of me, which those around him soon knew. I do not know how matters will end with me, for I was

too outspoken at Cairo to have strengthened
my position. When one depends on one man,
a bit of cheese or a fig will cause, perhaps, a
change in that man's digestion and temper."

Instead of returning to Khartoum direct,
after this abortive journey to Cairo, he determined to visit first the south-eastern districts
of his vast province, the littoral region beyond
the Straits of Bab-el Mandeb.

Zeila, the port of Harrar, was his first landing
place. Zeila, and the country about it, had
been ceded to the Khedive by Turkey for the
consideration of £15,000 a year additional
tribute. At Harrar, 200 miles inland, the
Governor was an old friend of Gordon—the
same Raouf Pasha whom he had found at
Gondokoro four years previously, and had then
deposed. " I am going to turn him out again,"
writes Gordon serenely; "he seems to be a
regular tyrant." The "regular tyrant" subsequently became Gordon's successor in the
governor-generalship of the Soudan. It was an
abominable journey, eight days long, from Zeila
to Harrar. Gordon learned that from the ports
of this coast, Zeila, Berberah, &c., the Mussulman population were continually passing slaves

across to Hodeidah on the Arabian coast opposite—a commerce which he determined to stop.
On his way to Harrar, he met a convoy of
£2,000 wòrth of coffee which Raouf was ex-
porting to Aden on his private account, meaning with the proceeds to purchase merchandise
which he would retail to the soldiers at Harrar
at exorbitant rates. This consignment Gordon
promptly confiscated, and Raouf, who he had
learned had " taken possession " of Harrar for
the Khedive by the effective measure of stran-
gling the old Ameer, accepted his fate at Gordon's
hands and went away quietly. Gordon followed him almost immediately, and by the end
of May had reached Khartoum, travelling viâ
Souakim and Berber. The alteration in his
relations with the Khedive, consequent on what
had occurred during his Cairo visit, had made
him simply a more uncompromising reformer
and disciplinarian. " I now only look to bene-
fiting the peoples," he wrote in alluding to the
changed attitude of the Khedive. It was in this
spirit, probably, that within the month after
his leaving Cairo, he had turned out three
Generals of Division, one General of Brigade,
and four Lieutenant-Colonels. For many months

after his return to Khartoum he continued in
residence there, engaging himself in questions
of finance, and the general settlement of the
affairs of the Province. The Soudanese railway had been in course of construction when
he entered on his governorship. The idea in
the abstract was excellent; the mistake was
that Ismail was so bent on bringing the
Soudan traffic down through Egypt that he
ignored the natural outlet of the trade to the
Red Sea by the Berber-Souakim route. Fifty
miles of line of railway had already been made
from Wadi Walfa towards Hanneck, at a cost
of nearly half a million sterling. Gordon's plan
was to complete the communication with Hanneck partly by tramway, partly by small steamers,
at a comparatively low expenditure, but his
project was not taken up, and there is the
section of railway to this day, out there in the
desert absolutely in the air. The Soudan
finances were not cheerful. On the previous
year there had been a deficit of £250,000, and
the budget for the current year did not balance
by £72,000. But the slave trade was being
resolutely hunted—in July Gordon records that
twelve slave caravans had been taken in two

months. At length, in December, he had Walad
el Michael off his shoulders. That worthy had
gone from Bogos with 300 men to make his
submission to King Johannis. That submission could not have been a pleasant ceremony.
Gordon thus describes it:—" He (Walad) will
have to pick up a big stone and put it on his
neck and go before the king thus. He will
then lie down before the throne. The king,
if he means to pardon him, will tell one of his
officers, 'Touch him with your hand on the
neck.' If he does not mean to do so, he says
'Touch him on the neck with your foot;' that
means the affair is not settled. Then come
pourparlers, &c., and Walad el Michael is either
imprisoned on a mountain that has no exit from
it but where there is water, or is pardoned."
Johannis himself still smarted under the insult-
ing fashion in which he considered the Khedive
had treated the envoy he had sent to Cairo.
But with his "beloved friend" Gordon, whom
he designated "Sultan of Soudan," he would
make peace, and with this intent he sent the
son of his Prime Minister, whom Gordon went
to meet at Katarif, received him with a salute
of artillery, and sent Mr. Winstanley back with

him to Abyssinia with presents for the king. The envoy drank half a bottle of cognac during a morning visit he paid to an Abyssinian lady married to one of Gordon's officers.

In February, 1879, there reached Gordon one of several summonses to Cairo, to be examined on Soudan affairs before the Council of Ministers. He refused to go, urging the necessity of remaining in the Soudan until the taxes for the past year had been collected, and until a revolt which had occurred in the Bahr Gazelle had been suppressed. This revolt had broken out in the previous July, and was a very serious matter. While Gordon had been keeping the slavers in check in the northern part of his huge territory, the slave-raiding scoundrelism of the Shakka nest had gathered head under the "cub" Suleiman, and were overrunning the Bahr Gazelle country. Gordon's work at Khartoum engrossed himself, but he acted with decision. He confiscated all the property of the Zebehr family, and having had good experience how able and resolute a man was his subordinate Gessi, he sent him south with an expeditionary force. Gessi had no easy enterprise. First, he had to go up into the Equato-

rial Province and bring down reinforcements.
Then the flooded country kept him inactive till
November. Suleiman meanwhile had not been
idle. He had proclaimed himself Lord of the
Province, and had surprised and massacred an
Egyptian garrison at Dem Idris. This feat
brought him support from the so-called neutral
Arab tribes ; he could control some 6,000 men,
and was reported to intend taking the initiative
and attacking Gessi in Rumbehk. Gessi, for
his part, was very weak, with but 300 regulars,
two guns, and 700 wretched irregulars. His
appeal to Gordon for aid was delayed by the
" sudd " in the river, and did not reach Khartoum for five months. But Gessi did not
wait for a reply from Khartoum. His men had
been deserting, but floggings and executions
cured that propensity, and in November he took
the offensive in a curiously amphibious march.
Tramping, rafting, and boating, he reached
the Waw in the beginning of December to find
the inhabitants bitterly incensed against the
slave-dealers, who had kidnapped from the district upwards of 10,000 women and children.
It was natural that he should here receive
local reinforcements, and with these he moved

westward to Dem Idris, the military station
which Suleiman had captured and destroyed.
Suleiman himself was leisurely marching towards
his "den" at Shakka, cumbered with his live
booty, but when he heard that Gessi had overcome the natural obstacles of the march from
Rumbehk, and was actually at Dem Idris, he
turned aside to attack him with 10,000 men.
The attack occurred on December 28th, and the
fighting was stubborn and bloody. Four times
did the slave crew charge Gessi's entrench-
ments, four times were they driven back, and
finally Suleiman retired with heavy loss. But
he would not own himself worsted, and Gessi
was too weak to improve his advantage; so a
fortnight later, having been strongly reinforced,
Suleiman assailed again. Two days' desperate
fighting compelled his retirement a second time,
but a third and fourth time he renewed the
struggle, and with no better result, notwithstanding that Gessi's ammunition was running
short. At length Gessi, having received some
ammunition, thought himself justified in taking
the offensive. On March 11th (1879), he
attacked Suleiman's camp of wooden huts connected by barricades of tree trunks. This

combustible position he set fire to with rockets ;
the slavers had to sally out as the only alternative to being roasted, and Gessi punished them
heavily, although his scantiness of ammunition
deterred him from an energetic pursuit. But
he was able to effect much. The slavers fled
to Dem Suleiman, three days' journey further
west, and Gessi swept the vicinity of Dem Idris
clear of them, liberated 10,000 of their victims,
and restored so great confidence that the tribes
were readily reinforcing him.

Down at Khartoum Gordon was asking for
bread in the shape of a regiment wherewith to
strengthen Gessi, and Cairo was offering him a
stone in the shape of Zebehr, the father of the
young fellow who was fighting with Gessi—the
man who, it was well known to the Khedive,
" had egged on his people to this revolt, had
caused the devastation of the whole country,
and who was alone responsible for the slave-
trade of the last ten years." Gordon would
not have Zebehr then at any price; yet it is
this man, whom Gordon himself has accused
and proven guilty of every atrocity, this man
whom he was sorry he had not the opportunity
to hang, to whom he now incomprehensibly

desires to entrust the future of the Soudan!
At length the Khedive gave Gordon permission to go up to Shakka and give the hand of
co-operation to Gessi. He left Khartoum early
in March, determined to break Shakka up
entirely, and evacuate it. This was his last
journey, and he hurried along with all his old
energy, detecting slave convoys as he moved.
" I smell slaves : look under those trees ! " he
exclaimed one morning to his secretary as they
rode along. " No," said the secretary; but the
slaves were there all the same, crouched down
in the long grass at the command of the ras-
cally Bashi-Bazooks who were driving them.
These miscreants were stripped, beaten, and
dismissed. " It was only," says Gordon,
grimly, " the want of power and legality which
prevented them being now on their backs looking up at the skies, for I had every wish to
shoot them." All the way along this march he
was releasing slaves whom he found being
driven down ; but the commerce continued of
so great dimensions as proved it was only
checked, not killed. " We must have caught,"
says he, " over 2,000 in less than nine months,
and I expect we did not catch one-fifth of the

caravans." At Edowa "a party of seven slave-dealers with twenty-three slaves were brought to me. Nothing could exceed the misery of these poor wretches. Some were children of not more than three years of age: they had come across that torrid zone from Shakka, a journey from which I on my camel shrank." And again: "When I had just begun this letter another caravan with two slave-dealers and seventeen slaves was brought in, and I hear others are on the way. Some of the poor women were quite nude. Both those caravans came from Shakka, where I mean to make a clean sweep of the slave-dealers."

All his thoughts during his long camel-rides were concentrated on devising methods to abolish this atrocious traffic. A scheme dawned upon him one night. He recognized that as all slaves coming from the south-west—he had pretty well closed the Equatorial route—must pass through Darfour to get into the Soudan, he could secure the control of Darfour by two simple regulations: 1. That all persons residing in Darfour must have a *permis de séjour;* and, 2. That all persons travelling to and from Darfour must have passports for themselves and their belongings. All infractions of those regulations he would punish with imprisonment and confiscation of property. But the millstone of Egypt and the Egyptians was round his neck. There stared him in the face the Khedive's firman declaring slave-dealing punishable only with imprisonment of from five months to five years, and Nubar had not long before telegraphed to him bluntly that the purchase and sale of slaves in Egypt was legal. He was straining every effort against the abomination, but, after all, it was like punching at a sack.

On his way up he had heard from Gessi, under date February 24th, asking for ammunition and troops, which Gordon hoped to send him up immediately on reaching Shakka. But a day before he reached Shakka he had further news from Gessi. That valiant man no more wanted assistance. He had done his work with the means to his hand. How he did it was thus. Suleiman was in Dem Suleiman, a place named in his own honour. On that place Gessi marched on Mayday. Three days later he was within striking distance, and he assaulted with such success that Suleiman

narrowly escaped capture, and a large booty
fell to Gessi. Like a bloodhound Gessi went
on the trail of the slave-prince, with 600 men
at his back, and resolute eagerness in his heart.
The country was ghastly with the fresh traces
of destruction ; the tropical rains had set in,
and in the long tramp his men all but starved.
At length a dense forest was reached, the heart
of which Gessi penetrated, only to be told by a
child whom he found the sole occupant of the
burnt forest-village, that Suleiman had spent the
previous night there. On he went in keen pursuit, the scent now hot, and next night a strange
thing happened. Scouts came to him who had
mistaken his camp for that of Rabi, Suleiman's
ally. They came, said they, from a force
Sultan Idris was bringing up, and begged the
supposititious Rabi to delay his advance until a
junction might be effected.

Gessi's manœuvring was brilliant. He
marched at once, struck Rabi at daylight, and
utterly routed him. Then he cleared the
field, camped, displayed Rabi's ensign he had
captured, and sent out emissaries to fall in Idris'
way and guide him to the camp of his friend
Rabi. His own force he ambushed in the grass

around the camp. Idris approached, and a
sudden storm caused his troops to hurry
forward in disorder to the shelter that seemed
awaiting them. Gessi's ambush spoke, and to
such purpose that only Idris and a few followers
escaped, all his property remaining in Gessi's
hands, who returned to Dem Suleiman laden
with spoil.

Gordon spread dismay at Shakka when he
announced his intention to clear out the place.
But he had begun to ask himself questions.
" I doubt much," said he "the liberation of the
slaves in the twelve years (according to the
convention) of which there now remains nine.
Who will do it?" Is he answering that question now with Zebehr, or will he answer it by
devoting himself to the great work? He was
anticipating the action that the resolution of
the British Government enforced, as the consequence of Hicks' defeat. "The Government
of the Egyptians in those far off countries is
nothing else but one of brigandage of the very
worst description. It is so bad that all hope of
ameliorating it is hopeless ; so I am doing the
only thing possible, that is, vacate them. I
have given up blaming the governors, for it is

o

useless, so I send them to Cairo. . . . . If you put aside the suppression of the slave-trade . . . . I have no hesitation in saying that an Arab governor suits the people better, and is more agreeable to them than an European." Has then Gordon sadly seen that the suppression of the slave-trade has now to be put aside, and so that Zebehr is the Arab governor the Soudan would prefer to him? There is another alternative, that which he outlined five years ago. " I declare if I could stop this traffic I would willingly be shot this night; this shows my ardent desire; and yet, strive as I can, I can scarcely see any hope of arresting the evil. Now comes the question. Could I sacrifice my life and remain in Kordofan and Darfour? I feel, if I could screw my mind up to it, I could cause the trade to cease, for its roots are in these countries." Omnipotent in the Soudan, unhampered by Egyptian intrigue and double dealing, what might not Gordon do!

Suleiman had had the effrontery to send emissaries to him, one of whom was Zebehr's chief secretary, the others long offenders. These emissaries Gordon tried by court-martial, and shot them. Stern measures were needed to support Gessi and scare the slave-dealers, who were now everywhere dispersing. As for the wretched slaves, they, thus released, were wandering about the country in thousands, and were " being snapped up by the native Arabs as if they were sheep." As he marched to Toashia to break up a slave gang there, the road he travelled was strewn with the skulls of wretches who had fallen out of the slave caravans and died by the wayside.

At Toashia Gessi and Gordon met, and the latter bestowed well-earned praises on his energetic lieutenant. When Gessi started on his mission of following up Suleiman to the bitter end, he went away a Pasha, decorated with the Osmanlie, and the possessor of the honorarium of £2,000. The finale of Gessi's work must be told in a sentence. With 300 men he surrounded a village in which Suleiman lay with 700. Gessi played the high game and gave Suleiman ten minutes to surrender, which he did. He and ten of his slaver comrades Gessi shot by Gordon's orders. The papers found on his son compromised the father so deeply that his trial became a necessity. Zebehr's guilt was proved, and he was sentenced to death. This is the man whom the Khedive pensioned, and to whose elevation to the governor-generalship of the Soudan England has been asked to consent. "What pensions—" asked Mr. Birkbeck Hill before the latter proposal was mooted,—"what pensions have the widows and orphans whom Zebehr has made by the thousand? What allowance have the poor worn out bodies of men, strong enough till he dragged them from their homes, who are now draining the last bitter dregs of life in cruel slavery? What recompense has been made to those whose bleached bones mark the track of his trade over many and many a league of ground?"

It was at Fogia, on July 1st, 1879, while on his way back to Khartoum, that Gordon received a telegram from Cherif Pasha, informing him of Ismail's abdication, and instructing him to proclaim throughout the Soudan that the Sultan had bestowed the Khedivial dignity on Tewfik Pasha. He obeyed the mandate, and formally acknowledged the communication, "nothing more." Before leaving Khartoum for Cairo, he received intelligence from Darfour that Haroun had been killed and his forces dispersed, so that the pacification of the Soudan was complete when he left it. He wrote home that he hoped to be back soon in England, but might have to go first to Abyssinia, on a mission to Johannis, and the latter expectation was fulfilled.

He had conceived a regard for Ismail, notwithstanding the friction between them that often had irritated him. "It pains me," he wrote, "what sufferings my poor Khedive Ismail had to go through." In Cairo the pashas all thought he would be badly received by Tewfik, because of his friendship for "the Incurable." He had indeed reached Cairo "very cross at the dismissal of Ismail," declined the special train Tewfik had ordered him, and meant also not to accept quarters at the palace but to go to the hotel. But he thought he "would not be justified in such a snub," so he went to the palace, and almost immediately was sent for by the new Khedive, whom he told he did not mean to return to the Soudan, but "would go to Massowah, settle with Johannis, and then go home." He and Tewfik did not get on very badly. "He told me," writes Gordon, "that my enemies with his father and with him had urged my dismissal ; that he had had terrible complaints against me, at which I laughed, and he did so also." And so he departed for Massowah *en route* for Abyssinia, leaving the warning that if on his return he heard any of the Council of Ministers had said anything against him, he would beg the Khedive, as a punishment equal to a sentence of death, to make the evil speaker governor-general of the Soudan. At Massowah he found that the Abyssinians were in virtual possession of Bogos, so that it was not a question of ceding or not ceding the country, but of retaking it. And, to add to his embarrassments, a telegram from the Khedive reached him just before he started inland that he was to cede nothing, but that he was to avoid a war. On the road he learnt that Walad el Michael had been made prisoner at Goura by Aloula, Johannis' lieutenant in chief. He himself was on his way first to Goura to see this Aloula. Although arrayed in marshal's uniform he met with scant respect, the soldiers scarcely acknowledging his salute. At length a shed of branches was reached, at the end of which was a couch on which lay a figure wrapped up in white, even to his face, the nose alone appearing. This was Aloula, and he was not sick. Gordon handed him the letter announcing the Khedive's accession and his own mission. This the Abyssinian received slightingly, putting the gold-tasselled green silk bag on the pistol lying by his side. Aloula once or twice broke the tedious silence by remarking, "You are English, and your nation are my brothers," but Gordon would not accept the overture, and claimed simply to be regarded as the Khedive's envoy and a Mussulman for the time. He was quartered close to Aloula's shed, and when he went for a stroll was politely ordered back to his circle, so that virtually he was a prisoner. Conscious that Egypt had treated Abyssinia very badly and unjustly, he took no umbrage at this treatment, which rather seems, indeed, to have amused him. The issue of his palavers with Aloula was that he undertook to see Johannis, Aloula agreeing not to attack Egypt during his absence. So Gordon started on his twelve days' journey to Debra Tabor, near Gondar, where Johannis was. It was an atrocious road he travelled by, sent by it to prevent his acquiring a knowledge of the better one which existed. The King, seated on a raised dais,

received him civilly enough, telling him the
cannon salute was in his honour, and then sent
him to his quarters in some wretched huts.
Next day Gordon had his audience. The King
recited his grievances against Egypt, and
Gordon made no demur. Then he formulated
his demands. They were at least comprehen-
sive. He demanded " the retrocession of
Metemna, Changallas, and Bogos, cession of the
ports of Zeila and Amphila, an Abouna, and
a sum of money of from one to two million
pounds." As alternatives he would accept
Bogos, Massowah, and the Abouna, adding
" I could claim Dongola, Berber, Nubia, and
Sennaar, but will not do so." Gordon asked the
King to put those demands into writing, and
give the Khedive six months to reply, to which
his Majesty consented, Gordon adding that,
personally, he did not think they would be complied with. The King's request was that
Gordon should accompany him to some baths,
two days distant, but the latter preferred waiting till his Majesty's return, a week later.
During the interval Gordon discovered that the
absurd claims had been inspired by the Greek
consul, and that hopes had been conceived of

detaching himself from the Khedive's interest. All that Gordon wanted was the letter the King had promised to write, and he was promised for the 8th (November) a farewell audience, when he should receive the letter. The interview is unique. Let Gordon himself recount it :

"KING (*very sulky*). 'Have you anything to say ?'

"GORDON. 'No.'

"KING. 'Go back to your master. I will send a letter.'

"GORDON. 'Will you give me the Egyptian soldiers ?'

"KING (*furious*). 'Why do you ask me this? you keep many of my subjects prisoners !'

"GORDON. 'No, every one is free.. Ask the Consul.'   [*Consul silent.*

"KING. 'I have written one letter, and I will write another about this. Go.' "

So Gordon left the presence, and started an hour afterwards. Just as he was starting, the interpreter brought him the letter, and a money present, which he, of course, sent back. He opened the letter, and, sure that it was too short to include the demands the King had specified,

had it translated. It ran thus :—"I have received the letters you sent me by *that man.* I
will not make a secret peace with you. If you
want peace, ask the Sultans of Europe." The
"that man," is an accepted expression of angry
contempt. On his way back to the coast Gordon was bullied, evilly entreated, and arrested
over and over again by Abyssinian soldiers, as
well as by the population. He suffered gross
indignities, and had to disburse a large sum in
bribes to obtain his extrication. At length he
reached Massowah, and rejoiced to see there
the English gunboat "Seagull." The Khedive
had ignored his request, made by telegraph when
he had been actually a prisoner, that a regiment
and war steamer should be sent to Massowah.
"I do not," he concludes, "write the details of
my misery. They are over, thank God. Sleep-
ing with an Abyssinian at the foot, and one on
each side of you, is not comfortable, and so I
passed my last night in Abyssinia."

He had sent in his resignation to the Khedive on his way back to Egypt. Probably he
had so only anticipated his dismissal. The
Pashas hated him and intrigued against him ;
Tewfik is but a poor weak creature. The ex-

pressions in his acceptance of Gordon's resignation were probably "from the teeth outwards."
" I should have liked to retain your services, but
in view of your persistent tender of resignation,
am obliged to accept it. I regret, my dear
Pasha, losing your co-operation, and in parting
with you, must express my sincere thanks to
you, assuring you that the remembrance of you
and your services to the country will outlive
your retirement." So Gordon turned his back
on the Soudan ; but he had not yet seen the last
of that region.

CHAPTER V.

" IT was none too soon," writes Mr. Birkbeck Hill, "that Colonel Gordon brought his work to an end and came home. Even his iron frame and unconquerable will must soon have given way under the vast strain that had been so long upon him. He had indeed ruled the great country over which he had been set. On his shoulders each man's burden lay, and such a burden had brought, as it ever must, dangers, troubles, cares, and sleepless nights. He had been ill—very ill, as some of his letters show—when he set out on his mission to Abyssinia. The hard usage which he had undergone, and the risks he had run in that kingdom, had still more tried his health. On his return to Alexandria, he was examined by Dr. Mackie, the surgeon to the British Consulate, who certified that he was 'suffering from symptoms of ner-

vous exhaustion, and alteration of the blood, giving rise to hæmorrhagic (purpuric) spots on the
skin, or cicatrices of former sores or wounds. I
have recommended him,' added Dr. Mackie,
'to retire for several months for complete rest
and quiet, and that he may be able to enjoy
fresh and wholesome food, as I consider that
much of what he is suffering from is the effect
of continued bodily fatigue, anxiety, and indi-
gestible food. I have insisted on his abstaining
from all exciting work—especially such as im-
plies business or political excitement."

This advice chimed aptly with Gordon's own
aspirations as to the life he would lead when
the wished-for retirement should at length come
to him. He had pictured in his quaint way the
restful life. He would lie in bed till noon; take
daily short strolls; never go on a railway journey, and never accept an invitation to dinner.
He meant to have oysters for lunch. The
oysters, perhaps, he obtained, but not the rest.
In May, 1881, the Marquis of Ripon was sailing for India to succeed Lord Lytton in the
Viceregal rule. There was the general realisation that India needed a strong moral tonic after
a *régime* so enervating and deteriorating. Lord

Ripon's character augured well for this wholesome process of deodorisation, and it may
have seemed to him that his hands would be
strengthened by the co-operation of such a man
as Gordon in the capacity of private secretary,
a position in many respects analogous to that of
prime minister. The offer of the post was
made to Gordon, and he accepted it in the
purest single-heartedness.   The appointment
astonished most those who knew India best.
Had Gordon entered into harness, he would
have done incalculable harm in his energetic
efforts to do good.   British India is a network
of cliquism and favoritism.   It is the peculiarity
of its administration that the very abuses pro-
duce a fairly good governing machinery, better
suited perhaps to the circumstances than would
a rule strung to a loftier key.   But Gordon was
not the man to have accepted the *laissez faire*
tone of the Anglo-Indian Raj : to put the matter
in the bluntest familiar phrase, he would have
been in India a bull in a china-shop.   The
realisation of the impossibility of the position
came to him on the voyage out, and on arriving
in Bombay he resigned the appointment.   Nothing need be added to the explanation of the

motives which led him to take this step, published by him in the Anglo-Indian newspapers.
—"Men, at times, owing to the mysteries of
Providence, form judgments which they afterwards repent of. This was my case in accepting the appointment Lord Ripon honoured me
in offering me. I repented of my act as soon
as I had accepted the appointment, and I
deeply regret that I had not the moral courage
to say so at that time. Nothing could have:
exceeded the kindness and consideration with
which Lord Ripon has treated me. I have
never met anyone with whom I could have felt
greater sympathy in the arduous task he has
undertaken." In a private letter he speaks
with yet greater frankness. "In a moment of
weakness," he writes, "I took the appointment
of private secretary to Lord Ripon, the new
Governor-General of India. No sooner had I
landed in Bombay than I saw that, in my irre-
sponsible position, I could not hope to do anything to the purpose, in the face of the vested
interests out there. Seeing this, and seeing
moreover, that my views were so diametrically
opposed to those of the official classes, I resigned. Lord Ripon's position was certainly a

great consideration with me. It was assumed
by some that my views of the state of affairs
were the Viceroy's; and thus I felt that I
should do him harm by staying with him.
We parted perfect friends. The brusqueness
of my leaving was inevitable, inasmuch as my
stay would have put me in possession of secrets
of state, that—considering my decision eventually to leave—I ought not to know. Certainly I might have stayed for a month or two,
had a pain in the hand, and gone quietly; but the
whole duties were so distasteful that I felt, being
pretty callous as to what the world says, that it
was better to go at once."

He resigned the Indian private secretaryship
on June 3rd, and had projected a journey to Zanzibar to help Sultan Syed Burghash in his work
of stopping the slave-trade, when there came to
him a request that he should visit China, between which Empire and Russia hostile differ-
ences threatened in connection with Kashgar.
The invitation came to him from his old friend,
Mr. Hart, the Chinese Commissioner of Customs,
and its terms ran thus : " I am directed to in-
vite you here (China). Please come and see
for yourself. This opportunity for doing really

useful work on a large scale ought not to be
lost. Work, position, conditions, can all be
arranged with yourself here to your satisfaction."
Gordon never learned by whom it was that
Mr. Hart had been directed to send him this invitation ; but there is little doubt that it emanated
from the Imperial Court. The Chinese cour-
tiers were keen for war; Gordon's old friend,
the "Governor Li" of the Tai-ping Rebellion
period, now in effect Prime Minister of China,
stood almost alone in urging the wisdom of
peace. What probably inspired the request for
Gordon's visit was, that he should give his
advice whether for peace or war; and that if
there should be war, he, being on the spot,
might be induced to take the command. He
saw his way to be of service to China, and he
telegraphed that he would come on by first opportunity. "As for conditions Gordon indifferent," was the characteristic postscript. But
he had to apply for leave to the Home Government, and when asked to state "more specifically" his purpose in going to China, and the
position he was to hold, all he could reply was
"I am ignorant." To simplify matters, he for-
warded to the War Office the resignation of his

P

commission and sailed for China. Gordon has ever received almost indulgent consideration from the military authorities at home, and his resignation was not accepted. He received permission to visit China on condition that he should accept no military service. He did not pledge himself not to do so, but explained that his efforts would be directed toward the preservation of peace. " My fixed desire," he said, " is to persuade the Chinese not to go to war with Russia, both in their own interests and those of the world, and especially those of England. To me it appears that the questions in dispute cannot be of such vital importance that an arrangement could not be come to by concessions on both sides. Whether I succeed in being heard or not is not in my hands. I protest, however, against being regarded as one who wishes for war in any country, far less in China. In the event of war breaking out, I could not answer how I should act for the present; but I shall ardently desire a speedy peace. Inclined as I am, with only a small degree of admiration for military exploits, I esteem it a far greater honour to promote peace than to gain any petty honours in a wretched war."

He left India for China on June 10th, went up from Hong Kong to Tientsin, and there had an interview with his old friend the statesman Li ; who when he saw him fell on his neck and kissed him. The little episode when Gordon had been hot on his track revolver in hand, was not permitted to affect the mutual cordiality. As the outcome of that interview and of others, Gordon found it would be a wise precautionary measure to clear his decks for action. While a British officer he had not that full freedom of speech and action which he desiderated, so he sent this telegram to London : " July 27th, 1880. I have seen Li Hung Chang, and he wishes me to stay with him. I cannot desert China in her present crisis, and would be free to act as I think fit. I therefore beg to resign my commission in her Majesty's service."

But Gordon was not to be lost to her Majesty's service. Already, on August 14th, he was back in Shanghai, his work accomplished. He had brought to China real " Peace with honour." His counsels had turned the wavering scale, and the peace party in the Imperial Councils had conquered by virtue of the weight of the arguments he embodied in a memorandum which is a model of condensed wisdom and lucidity. Its concluding words were these: "China wants no big officer from Foreign Powers; I say big officer, because I am a big officer in China. If I stayed in China, it would be bad for China, because it would vex the American, French, and German Governments, who would want to send their officers. Besides, I am not wanted. China can do what I recommend herself. If she cannot, I could do no good."

The resignation of his commission had been declined, but his leave had been cancelled. He was rather cavalier with the War Office people, and the constant consideration shown him is a sufficient answer to accusations which we have recently heard. In reply to the message which reached him at Shanghai, intimating non-acceptance of his resignation but the cancellation of his leave, he sent this brusque ultimatum: "You might have trusted me. My passage from China was taken before the arrival of telegram of August 14th, which states leave cancelled, &c. Do you still insist on rescinding the same?" The brief answer reached him

next day : " Leave granted to February 28th."
By that date he was back in England.

But not for long. He could anticipate ease,
but the crave to be doing something had so
overmastered him that he could not take that
ease when he might. He threw himself earnestly into the current questions of the hour,
and paid a visit to the King of the Belgians to
talk over an International Expedition to the
Congo, which King Leopold meditated despatching under his leadership. In May he was
on his way to the Mauritius to take up the duty
he had accepted there as Commanding Royal
Engineer. As he passed through Suez he visited
the grave of his gallant lieutenant, Gessi, who
was the latest victim to the horrible Soudan.
Gessi had died in the French Hospital at Suez
on 3rd April, " after protracted sufferings,
caused by the terrible privations in the previous
months of November and December, when he
had been shut in by the impassable ' sudd '
barrier in the Bahr Gazelle." Gordon remained
in his Mauritius post about ten months. " It
was," says Mr. Hake, "a happy and peaceful
time. He became deeply interested in the
Seychelles ; he made some curious researches

concerning the site of the Garden of Eden ; he planned and suggested certain excellent schemes for the defence of the Indian Ocean." On March 6th, it should have been said, he attained the rank of Major-General.

While Gordon was staying at Lausanne in the spring of 1881, he had received and had declined an offer from the Government of the Cape of Good Hope of the command of the Colonial forces, at a salary of £1,500 a year. He had made a tender of his services in a sphere of wider responsibility, to which the Colonial Ministers had apparently not seen their way to accede. But troubles had been thickening upon them since ; and they bethought themselves again of a man whose administrative genius stood so high. They applied to the Home Government for consent to utilise Gordon's services, and this accorded, the Premier of the Cape Government, on March 3rd, 1882, sent him the following communication : " Position of matters in Basutoland grave, and of utmost importance that Colony secure services of some one of proved ability, firmness, and energy. Government resolved therefore asking whether you are disposed to renew offer which you made to former Ministry. They do not expect you to be bound by salary then stated. Should you agree to place services at disposal of this Government, it is very important you should at once visit the Colony, in order to learn facts bearing on situation. Could you do this you would confer signal favour on Colony, leaving your future action unpledged. . . . It is impossible within limits telegram to enter fully into case, and in communication with you, Government rely upon same devotion to duty which prompted former offer, to excuse this sudden request." Gordon's former offer had been of "his services for two years to assist in terminating war and administering Basutoland."

He immediately took ship, and reached the Cape in May. Governor and Ministers found themselves in a difficulty. Mr. Orpen was Administrator of Basutoland, and him they were reluctant to remove. They wanted Gordon's services, yet they did not see how to utilise them, since Gordon and Orpen would clash. The object of the former in coming to the Cape was clear. He had once already declined the appointment simply of Commandant of the

Colonial Forces. He wished to engage himself
in the settlement of the Basutoland troubles,
and the Cape Government were anxious that
he should do so, but could not make up their
minds to clear the way for Gordon by the removal of Mr. Orpen. Most men in Gordon's
position would, under those circumstances, have
declined the Cape service altogether; but he,
hoping disinterestedly to find some method
whereby he might be of use, took the appointment of Commandant-General which he had
refused a year previously. It was told him
that the appointment was but a temporary expedient. He studied the native problem carefully, and sent in a memorandum giving as his
opinion that the Basutos should have been con-
sulted as to their transference from the Imperial
to the Cape Government, and suggesting that
they should be summoned to a conference concerning the terms of agreement with the colonial Government. To this memorandum no
reply was accorded, and Gordon proceeded up
country to King William's Town, and there
prepared the report on the Colonial forces
which the Premier had requested of him. It
was full of suggestions for reforms, and Gordon

showed how the Colony could, by the adoption of economies he pointed out, maintain an army 8,000 strong, instead of the existing force of 1,600, at an expense of £7,000 less than the smaller force cost. Neither on this, nor on suggestions in regard to other matters which he had been asked to make, did any action follow. In July the Government requested him to visit Basutoland, to which his reply, accompanied by a memorandum as to the line of action he would recommend there, was that there was no use in his going to Basutoland, unless the Government were prepared to acknowledge his presence and take account of his proposals. To this, apparently, the Government did not see their way, and Gordon remained at his military post in King William's Town, until next month, when the Cape Secretary for Native Affairs came up and requested him to accompany him into Basutoland, whither Mr. Sauer was going to see Mr. Orpen, the Ministerial representative. Gordon demurred. He pointed out that he was opposed to Mr. Orpen's policy, and could do no good; but Sauer pleaded hard, and he went. As the issue, Gordon became more and more con-

vinced of the futility of a policy which consisted in trying to settle matters by using one
set of Basutos to coerce another, and wrote a
memorandum embodying his opinions. Then
Mr. Sauer asked him to go, as a private indi-
vidual, to Masupha, the hostile Basuto chief,
and try to win him over. Gordon went with
neither credentials ' nor instructions, on an
errand of no inconsiderable risk. Masupha,
fortunately, was a gentleman, although a
" nigger." While Gordon was negotiating
with him in the name of the Cape Government, the emissaries of that Government inspired Letsea, the opposition Basuto Chief, to
assail Masupha. The latter might have held
Gordon as a hostage; instead, he magnani-
mously allowed him to go in peace.

Conduct of this description Gordon, with all
his self-abnegation, was not the man to brook.
The moment he got back from Masupha into
what of civilisation South Africa anywhere
affords, he telegraphed to Cape Town : " As I
am in a false position here, and am likely to do
more harm than good, I propose leaving for
the Colony, and when I have finished some
Reports I will come down to Cape Town,

when I trust Government will accept my resignation." The reply was : " The Premier has no objection to your coming to Cape Town as proposed." But Gordon had taken service under certain conditions which he was prepared to fulfil, and intimated accordingly. The Premier was severe in a Little Peddlington fashion, but after the same fashion grandly magnanimous. This was his reply : " In answer to your telegram proposing to come to Cape Town and expressing a wish that Government would accept your resignation, and to subsequent messages intimating that when you telegraphed it had escaped your memory that you had stated your willingness to remain until Parliament met, I have to state that I have no wish to hold you to your promise, and am now prepared to comply with the desire expressed, that your resignation should be accepted : after the intimation that you would not fight the Basutos, and considering the tenor of your communication with Masupha, I regret to record my conviction that your continuance in the position you occupy would not be conducive to public interest."

It was a minor thing to have earned the

gratitude of an Emperor for the subjugation of a rebellion that was striking at the vitals of his Empire; it was a trifle to have been Viceroy of the Soudan, and to have won the admiration of the world because of the resolute skill with which he had pacificated that vast and turbulent region. What availed Gordon all these things so long as he had been unsuccessful in giving satisfaction to the Premier of the Cape Colony? He has lived through much, through what would have proved fatal to most men; but the most surprising proof of tenacious vitality he has given is that he should have survived that august functionary's recorded conviction that his continuance in office "would not be conducive to public interest." He staggered back to England, there to recover from the prostration of despair. It is surprising, indeed, that, after so authoritative an imprimatur of his incapacity, wanton recklessness could tempt greater powers than the Cape Government to entrust him with responsibility. Yet this has been done.

CHAPTER VI.

Soon after his return to England from South Africa General Gordon went to Palestine, and settled outside Jerusalem. Mr. Hake throws some light into his life and aims during this year of repose. "Most of his time," writes that gentleman, "is devoted to research, and it is with an eagerness that is almost a passion that he pursues the survey of the Holy Sepulchre, the Tabernacle, and the walls of Jerusalem. . . . He has taken the holy sites in hand to prove them not the holy sites at all, greatly to the horror and scandal of clerical tourists. But he is no mere iconoclast; he works as one seeing sermons in stones and good in everything—with the faith of a Christian, but the eye and brain of an engineer. The Bible is his guide; and he 'does not care for sites if he has a map.' 'In reality,' he says,

' no man, in writing on those sites ought to draw on his imagination ; he ought to keep to the simple facts, and not prophecy, to fill up gaps.' . . . And his greatest interest of all, and his latest, is the proposed Jordan Canal ; and the thoroughness with which he has gone into the details of this enormous scheme is complete and unassailable."

But in Palestine Gordon was in retirement, and he is a man who has brought it upon himself that while his powers remain to him, there can be for him no prolonged retirement. There is no rest for a philanthropist of his energetic stamp.

If the Mahdi had asserted himself while Gordon was still Governor-General of the Soudan, it is not probable that the world would have heard much of him. But it was not until more than a year after Gordon had quitted Egypt, that Mahomet Ahmed began to put forward his divine commission. He had, nevertheless, been planning his crusade during Gordon's reign, although that satrap does not seem to have even heard of him. Mahomet Ahmed, whom we now know as "the Mahdi," is a native of the province of Dongola, and his father was a carpenter. He himself was apprenticed to an uncle whose trade was that of a boatman, but he ran away from that service, and became the disciple of a faki (head dervish) who lived near Khartoum. As the result of a close study of religion, he was himself made a faki, and in 1870 took up his residence on the island of Abba, near Kana, on the White Nile. He speedily began to acquire a reputation for great devoutness, and so became wealthy, gathered disciples, and married freely, selecting wives from the families of the most influential sheikhs of the vicinity. In the early part of 1881, Gordon having gone, he began to assert the claim that he was "the Mahdi," the long-expected redeemer of Islam whom Mahomet had foretold, and claiming a divine commission to reform Islam, and establish an universal equality, an universal law, an universal religion, and a community of goods. Setting himself to gather about him a following, he addressed appeals to his brother fakis, one of whom informed the Government of his schemes and pretensions, adding the belief that he was a madman. Raouf Pasha, the then Governor of the Soudan, proceeded to take cognisance of him as the result of this information ; and it is at this stage of his career that the Mahdi steps out into the arena of contemporary history. Colonel Stewart thus characterises him :—" In person the Mahdi is tall and slim, with a black beard, and a light brown complexion. Like most Dongolawis, he reads and writes with difficulty. Judging from his conduct of affairs and policy I should say he has considerable natural ability. The manner in which he has managed to merge together the usually discordant tribes denotes great tact. He probably had been preparing the movement for some time." Colonel Stewart in another portion of his report gives some indication of the reason why a religious fanatic finds so readily a following in the Soudan :— " The Arabs and Dongolawis," he writes, " negroes, and others settled within the Arab (the northern) zone of the Soudan, are all Mohammedans of the Maliki school. This religion, however, owing to the prevailing ignorance of the people, partakes mostly of an emotional and superstitious nature. Hence the enormous influence of the fakis or spiritual leaders, who are credited with a supernatural power, and are almost more venerated than the Prophet."

Another cause for the strength of the Mahdi's following seems to have been that the great slaveowners—the sheikhs and chiefs who had flourished on their nefarious practices under Zebehr, and whom all the efforts of Baker and Gordon had not put down—threw in their lot eagerly with any enterprise that struck at the Egyptian rule, under which a term had been definitely fixed for the emancipation of the slaves.

The Mahdi easily repulsed the detachment Raouf Pasha sent out to bring him in, and at the end of 1881 defeated in the most summary style a stronger force under Rashid Bey that had been despatched to drive him out of Gabel Gadir. But these were petty successes compared with the great victory he gained in June 1882 over the main Egyptian army of the Soudan, which Abdul Kadir, who had superseded Raouf Pasha, had gathered for the purpose of crushing him, and the command of which had been entrusted to Yussuf Pasha. Very few of the Egyptian soldiers escaped, and all their commanders were slain. Thus early did the Arab fanaticism display itself. The attack at Gabel Geon was led by the dervishes, headed by an enthusiast of exceptional dash and fury,

Q

who was known as " The Dervish," and of whose conduct Colonel Stewart reported : " I hear that the desperate and fearless way in which he rushes on a square armed with Remingtons is something marvellous."

After his victory at Gabel Geon, the Mahdi pursued the offensive. He overran the open country unchecked, but failed to achieve any success against places that had been fortified, even though the fortifications were feeble. In assailing El Obeid, he met with a severe repulse, losing 6,000 of his warriors in one assault alone. During the months of the campaign which the battle of Tel-el-Kebir ended so summarily, there were discrepant rumours concerning affairs in the Soudan. Now there were reports of the dispersal of the Mahdi's bands ; reports, again, of their threatening Khartoum and the towns on the White Nile. Then later, in the winter season of 1882-3, came definite tidings of the surrender to the Mahdi of the town of El Obeid, after the garrison had endured desperate straits. The surrender, however, once consummated, most of the garrison, with the Commandant Iskander Bey at their head, took service under their conqueror. With the proverbial zeal of the rene-gade, Iskander Bey became the medium for endeavouring to gain over officers in the Egyp-tian army in which he had himself held a com-mission. After the fall of El Obeid the Mahdi remained himself inside the Kordofan Province, but his emissaries were active in other parts of the Soudan.

The grave situation in Lower Egypt had distracted attention from what was happening in the Soudan, but as soon as might be after the reconstruction following on Arabi's collapse, preparations began for the renewal of operations against the Mahdi. Colonel Hicks, an officer who had retired from the Indian Army after much and good service, was appointed to the expedition, at first in the nominal position of chief of the staff, and later he was made com-mander-in-chief. In the early summer of 1883, Hicks Pasha conducted a short and successful campaign in the Sennaar district (lying between the Blue Nile and the White Nile), against a section of the Mahdi's force, commanded by a lieutenant named Amed Mokushigi. While on the march for Gebel Ain, on the morning of April 29th, Hicks was furiously assailed. Time

had served him to form square, and in this attitude, halted, he awaited the attack. A military
correspondent of the *Daily News* vividly described the fight, and his account has a special
interest, as the first portrayal of that method of
attack which our soldiers had to encounter
later at El Teb and Tamanieb.

"We opened a tremendous fusillade from our
front face, apparently without effect, for still
they came on gallantly, but at 500 yards they
began to fall fast. Still the chiefs led on their
men with all the reckless and romantic chivalry
of the Saracen knights. One by one they fell
dismounted, two or three to rise again and dart
forward on foot, waving their standards, only to
drop and rise no more. After half an hour's
continuous rattle of musketry, seeing their chiefs
fallen and their banners in the dust, the advancing hordes waver, and are greeted with a
tremendous yell from our troops, who had
stood firmly and unflinchingly, and I may
say as steadily as any troops could. Now
the enemy move off to the right among the
long grass, and our front is cleared. Shells
burst among them. Soon all were out of sight,
except a few who walked about unconcernedly,

and actually singly came up, after the rest had retreated, to within a few yards, brandishing their spears in defiance. One after another those fanatics were shot down. . . . Nordenfeldts and Remingtons are no respecters of creeds or fanatical idiosyncrasies. Sheikh after sheikh had gone down with his banner, although the Mahdi had assured each he was invulnerable, and their faithful but misguided followers had fallen in circles around the chiefs they blindly followed. Twelve of the most prominent leaders—nine from Samoar and three from Kordofan—had left their bones to whiten on the field amidst three hundred of their followers."

The rainy season compelled Hicks to suspend active operations until the autumn, but on September 9th he moved out from El Duem on his fatal march on El Obeid. He himself had misgivings, and had applied for reinforcements which could not be given him. The Europeans who accompanied him were quite outspoken in their forebodings of disaster. Major Seckendorff wrote, " I have seen Egyptians in three battles, and should be at a loss to find one hero among them." Poor O'Donovan thus

adumbrated his fate—referring in a private
letter to the death of a friend, he continued—
" It would be odd if the next intelligence from
this part of the world told that I too had gone
the way of all flesh.   However, to die even out
here, with a lance-head as big as a shovel
through me, will meet my views better than the
slow, gradual sinking into the grave which is
the lot of so many.   You know I am by this
time, after an experience of many years, pretty
well accustomed to dangers of most kinds, yet
I assure you I feel it terrible to face deadly
peril far away from civilised ideas, and where no
mercy is to be met with, in company with fellows
that you expect to see run at any moment, and
who will leave you behind to face the worst."

The last word from the doomed column came
from that gallant ill-fated war correspondent in
a telegram from "Sange Hamferid Camp," forty-
five miles south-west of El Duem.   There is a
sough in its final words of the evil to come.
" We are running a terrible risk in abandoning
our communications and marching 230 miles
into an unknown country.   But we have burnt
our ships.   The enemy is still retiring and
sweeping the country bare of cattle.   The water

supply is the cause of intense anxiety. The camels are dropping." And so ended O'Donovan's work in the profession which he adorned; so closed, too, the scanty record of this fateful advance!

Authentic details may never be forthcoming of the stupendous catastrophe which befell Hicks' column; and a lurid cloud of mystery may hang over the last scenes for all time. No European present in the fighting that wrought its annihilation is known to have survived. The report that Mr. Vizetelly, the artist, had escaped death, seems untrue. We know absolutely nothing more authentically as to the details of the catastrophe than we did in November last. Of this we may be sure at least, that the handful of our countrymen died as beseemed men who had worn the British uniform.

The British Government had specifically refused to be accessory in any sense to the military doings in the Soudan undertaken for the subjugation of the Mahdi. On the contrary, so early as May, 1883, Lord Granville had carefully explained that "her Majesty's Government were in no way responsible for the operations in the Soudan, which had been undertaken on the authority of the Egyptian Government, or for the appointment or actions of General Hicks." It remains to be said that, since British influence was paramount at Cairo, a hint from Downing Street would have been sufficient to arrest the progress of operations of such manifest hazard, and an untoward issue to which could not fail to bring about momentous complications.

The mind of a government is like a snow-ball—*acquirit vires eundo;* but the resemblance is only to a very slow-rolling snow-ball. The news of the catastrophe to Hicks' column reached England about 20th November. Nearly a month later, Lord Granville had hardened his heart to "recommend" the Khedive's Ministers to resolve on the abandonment of the Soudan, and had intimated his Government's intention not to employ British or Indian troops in that province. The Egyptian Ministers were not unnaturally reluctant to fall in with this recommendation. Three weeks later Lord Granville hardened his heart somewhat further. He was not peremptory, but he directed Sir Evelyn Baring "to urge with all earnestness upon the Khedive and Ministers that all military operations, excepting those for the rescue of outlying garrisons, should cease in the Soudan." Later in the same day, he braced himself to be explicit. No longer did he "recommend," or "urge", the jelly had stiffened, and he now used the alarming word "insist." " It must be made clear," he telegraphed, "to the Egyptian authorities that the responsibility which for the time rests on England obliges her Majesty's Government to insist on the adoption of the policy which they recommend, and that it will be necessary that the ministers and governors who do not follow this course should cease to hold office." Whereupon the Cherif ministry resigned, the Khedive "accepted cordially the abandonment of the whole of the Soudan ; " Nubar Pasha succeeded Cherif, and "entirely concurred in the wisdom of abandoning the Soudan."

Her Majesty's Government might insist and the Khedive and his new ministers might consent, but of themselves these mental phenomena did not go a great way toward effecting the evacuation of the Soudan. It was studded all over from the Abyssinian frontier to Fascher,

by Egyptian garrisons all of which were lock-
fast in their stations, and what with troops,
officials, merchants, nondescripts, women and
children, the Egyptian population in the Soudan
numbered about 30,000. The delay of her
Majesty's Government in screwing itself up to
utter the word "insist" had materially added to
the difficulties of the extrication of these. Since
her ministers had at last uttered that strong
word not even a government with a genius
for evading responsibility could well deny that
England had incurred some responsibility in .
regard to those unfortunate derelicts of the
Egyptian *régime*. "We were all agreed," indeed said Mr. Gladstone, "that measures
should be taken for the relief of the garrisons."
Baker had gone to Souakim with several ship-
loads of poltroons, but that was not much of a
"measure." What other "measure" could the
ingenuity devise of a Government who had
definitely disavowed their intention of employing
their troops in the Soudan ?

On Saturday, January 19th, the nation
learned with a thrill of glad surprise that on
the previous evening General Gordon had left
England for the Soudan, having accepted the

mission "to report on the military situation there, to provide in the best manner for the safety of the European population of Khartoum, and of the Egyptian garrisons throughout the country, as well as for the evacuation of the Soudan with the exception of the seaboard." This was what the *Times* of that morning told us, and the sentiment of relief, pleasure, and pride was universal. To know that Gordon had gone, that was enough for most people. Mr. Gladstone afterwards in the •House of Commons, on the evening of February 12th, defined more closely the duty which Gordon had undertaken. "General Gordon went," said the Premier, "not for the purpose of reconquering the Soudan, or to persuade the chiefs of the Soudan—the Sultans at the head of their troops—to submit themselves to the Egyptian Government. He went for no such purpose as that. He went for the double purpose of evacuating the country, by extricating the Egyptian garrisons, and reconstituting it, by giving back to these Sultans their ancestral powers, withdrawn or suspended during the period of Egyptian occupation. General Gordon has in view the withdrawal from the country of no less than 29,000 persons under military service in Egypt, and the House will see how vast was the trust which was placed in the hands of this remarkable person. We cannot exaggerate the importance we attach to his mission. We are unwilling—I may say we were resolved to do nothing which should interfere with the pacific scheme, a scheme, be it remembered, absolutely the only scheme, which promised a satisfactory solution of the Soudanese difficulty by at once extricating the garrisons and reconstituting the country upon its old basis of local privileges."

I have spoken of the country's surprise at the sudden despatch of Gordon on this mission. And it was a genuine surprise. He left Charing Cross in the evening of 18th January. But it was known that on the previous day Gordon had arrived in Brussels to receive from the King of the Belgians his final instructions for the anti-slavery expedition to the headquarters of the Congo the command of which he had accepted. There had been hope till then that he might go to the Soudan, but with his departure for Brussels that hope had died. It had been in the minds of many ever since

the news came of Hicks' misfortune, but the
universality of the aspiration had been kindled
by an opportune stroke of journalistic perspi-
cacity. General Gordon, having travelled from
Palestine to Brussels, had come from Brussels
to England on the 7th of January, on a short
farewell visit to his sister at Southampton.
There, on the 8th, a representative of the *Pall
Mall Gazette* had an interview with him, the
publication of the notes of which "transformed
the whole situation." The conviction was universal that the striking paper in that journal
forced the hand of the Government; and probably remains so, in the face of Mr. Gladstone's
explanation that the Government had long previously entertained the desire to avail themselves of General Gordon's services, and that
the hindrance was the "aversion" of the Egyptian Government. It was at least a significant
coincidence that this aversion should have "become mitigated and at length entirely removed"
within a week of the publication in the *Pall
Mall Gazette* of its interview with General
Gordon. But for that interview and the
popular feeling it evoked, it seems highly probable that by this time General Gordon and

Mr. Stanley would have been discussing the former's programme on the banks of the Congo.

Whatever Gordon's own views were as to the policy which ought to be pursued in the Soudan, he loyally subordinated them to the instructions he took from the Ministers at that afternoon consultation on his arrival from Brussels. " I go to cut the dog's tail off. I've got my orders, and I'll do it, *coûte que coûte.*" At eight o'clock he started. " The scene at the station," said the *Pall Mall Gazette,* " was very interesting. Lord Wolseley carried the General's portmanteau, Lord Granville took his ticket for him, and the Duke of Cambridge held open the carriage door." His companion was Lieut.-Colonel Stewart, 11th Hussars.

The original intention was that General Gordon should go through the canal straight to Souakim, and thence attempt to reach Khartoum by the Berber route, relying for his safety in this hazardous enterprise on his old friendly relations with the Hadendoah tribes, who inhabit the country between Souakim and Berber. It was understood that he desired to maintain his independence unfettered by any relations with Egypt, and it was known that he had said stern things about the Khedive, who might, therefore, have a reluctance to meet him. Sir Evelyn Wood went down to Port Said to meet Gordon on his arrival there, and it was arranged that if he were firm in his resolve not to visit Cairo, but go straight through the canal, Sir Evelyn Baring was to go to Suez and have a conference with him there. But Colonel Harrington had come back from Souakim with an unfavourable report as to the practicability of the Souakim-Berber road, and, influenced doubtless by other reasons more than by this argument, Gordon altered his route so as to include Cairo, and reached that capital on the night of January 25, arriving, as his wont, in advance of the time at which he was expected. He was keen to push forward, and had desired to leave Cairo within twenty-four hours, but was prevailed on to stay a day longer, for many questions had to be discussed and many points settled. On the morning of the 26th he had an interview with the Khedive which was of a very cordial character, his Highness expressing great satisfaction that Gordon should have undertaken to go to the Soudan, and his com-

plete confidence in him. The day was consumed in conferences at the British Residency
with Sir Evelyn Baring, Nubar Pasha, Sir
Evelyn Wood, and others; and when Gordon
left Cairo on the 27th January he went not only
as British High Commissioner, but as the
Khedive's Governor-General of the Soudan.
He was accompanied by the son of the Sultan
of Darfour, to whom the Khedive, at Gordon's
suggestion, had restored, so far as he was concerned, the parental dominions, and General
Graham convoyed his old comrade as far as
Assouan. When they reached Korosko,
General Gordon and Colonel Stewart quitted
the Nile Valley and struck across the Nubian
Desert, on their camel ride of 240 miles to
Abou Hamed. They plunged into the desert
without any military escort, and a feverish
anxiety for their safety had to be endured for
nine days, since no sure news could be received
respecting them until they should have reached
Berber.

The following are the instructions from the
British Foreign Office under which General
Gordon had consented to go to the Soudan :—

"FOREIGN OFFICE, *Jan.* 18, 1884.

" SIR,—Her Majesty's Government are desirous that you should proceed at once to Egypt, to report to them on the military situation in the Soudan and on the measures which it may be advisable to take for the security of the Egyptian garri‑ sons still holding positions in that country, and for the safety of the European population in Khartoum. You are also desired to consider and report upon the best mode of effecting the eva‑ cuation of the interior of the Soudan, and upon the manner in which the safety and the good administration by the Egyptian Government of the ports on the sea coast can best be secured. In connection with this subject, you should pay especial con‑ sideration to the question of the steps that may usefully be taken to counteract the stimulus which it is feared may possibly be given to the slave trade by the present insurrectionary move‑ ment and by the withdrawal of the Egyptian authority from the interior. You will be under the instructions of her Majesty's Agent and Consul-General at Cairo, through whom your reports to her Majesty's Government should be sent under flying seal. You will consider yourself authorized and instructed to perform such other duties as the Egyptian Government may desire to entrust to you, and as may be communicated to you by Sir E. Baring. You will be accompanied by Colonel Stewart, who will assist you in the duties thus confided to you. On your arrival in Egypt you will at once communicate with Sir E. Baring, who will arrange to meet you, and will settle with you whether you should proceed direct to Suakin, or should go yourself or des‑ patch Colonel Stewart to Khartoum viâ the Nile.—I am, &c. (Signed) GRANVILLE."

During the leisure of his voyage across the Mediterranean, Gordon had written the following memorandum on these instructions, which was received by the Foreign Office on February 1st :—

" I understand that her Majesty's Government have come to the irrevocable decision not to incur the very onerous duty of

R

securing to the peoples of the Soudan a just future Government.
That, as a consequence, her Majesty's Government have determined to restore to these peoples their independence, and will
no longer suffer the Egyptian Government to interfere with their
affairs.

" 2. For this purpose her Majesty's Government have decided
to send me to the Soudan to arrange for the evacuation of
these countries, and the safe removal of the Egyptian employés
and troops.

" 3. Keeping paragraph No. 1 in view, viz., that the evacuation of the Soudan is irrevocably decided on, it will depend on
circumstances in what way this is to be accomplished.   My idea
is that the restoration of the country should be made to the different petty Sultans who existed at the time of Mehemet Ali's
conquest, and whose families still exist ; that the Mahdi should
be left altogether out of the calculation as regards the handing
over the country ; and that it should be optional with the
Sultans to accept his supremacy or not.   As these Sultans
would probably not be likely to gain by accepting the Mahdi as
their sovereign, it is probable that they will hold to their independent positions.   Thus we should have two factors to deal
with—namely, the petty Sultans asserting their several independence, and the Mahdi's party aiming at supremacy over them.
To hand, therefore, over to the Mahdi the arsenals, &c., would,
I consider, be a mistake.   They should be handed over to the
Sultans of the States in which they are placed.   The most difficult question is how and to whom to hand over the arsenals of
Khartoum, Dongola, and Kassala, which towns have, so to say,
no old standing families, Khartoum and Kassala having sprung
up since Mehemet Ali's conquest.   Probably it would be advisable to postpone any decision as to these towns till such time as
the inhabitants have made known their opinion.

" 4. I have in paragraph 3 proposed the transfer of the lands
to the local Sultans, and stated my opinion that these will not
accept the supremacy of the Mahdi.   If this is agreed to and my
supposition is correct as to their action, there can be but little doubt
that as far as he is able the Mahdi will endeavour to assert his
rule over them, and will be opposed to any evacuation of the
Government employés and troops.   My opinion of the Mahdi's

forces is, that the bulk of those who were with him at Obeid will refuse to cross the Nile, and that those who do so will not exceed 3,000 or 4,000 men, and also that these will be composed principally of black troops who have deserted, and who, if offered fair terms, would come over to the Government side. In such a case, viz., 'Sultans accepting transfer of territory and refusing the supremacy of the Mahdi, and Mahdi's black troops coming over to the Government,' resulting weakness of the Mahdi ; what should be done should the Mahdi's adherents attack the evacuating columns? It cannot be supposed that these are to offer no resistance, and if in resisting they should obtain a success, it would be but reasonable to allow them to follow up the Mahdi to such a position as would insure their future safe march. This is one of those difficult questions which our Government can hardly be expected to answer, but which may arise and to which I would call attention. Paragraph 1 fixes irrevocably the decision of the Government, viz., to evacuate the territory, and, of course, as far as possible involves the avoidance of any fighting. I can therefore only say, that having in view paragraph 1 and seeing the difficulty of asking her Majesty's Government to give a decision or direction as to what should be done in certain cases, that I will carry out the evacuation as far as possible according to their wish to the best of my ability, and with avoidance, as far as possible, of all fighting. I would, however, hope that her Majesty's Government will give me their support and consideration should I be unable to fulfil all their expectations.

" 5. Though it is out of my province to give any opinion as to the action of her Majesty's Government in leaving the Soudan, still I must say it would be an iniquity to reconquer these peoples and then hand them back to the Egyptians without guarantees of future good government. It is evident that this we cannot secure them without an inordinate expenditure of men and money. The Soudan is a useless possession, ever was so, and ever will be so. Larger than Germany, France, and Spain together, and mostly barren, it cannot be governed except by a Dictator who may be good or bad. If bad he will cause constant revolts. No one who has ever lived in the Soudan can escape the reflection, 'What a useless possession is this land.'

Few men also can stand its fearful monotony and deadly cli-mate.

" 6. Said Pacha, the Viceroy before Ismael, went up to the Soudan with Count F. de Lesseps. He was so discouraged and horrified at the misery of the people that at Berber Count de Lesseps saw him throw his guns into the river, declaring that he would be no party to such oppression. It was only after the urgent solicitations of European consuls and others that he recon-sidered his decision. Therefore, I think her Majesty's Govern-ment are fully justified in recommending the evacuation, inas-much as the sacrifices necessary towards securing a good government would be far too onerous to admit of such an at-tempt being made. Indeed one may say it is impracticable at any cost. Her Majesty's Government will now leave them as God has placed them ; they are not forced to fight among them-selves, and they will no longer be oppressed by men coming from lands so remote as Circassia, Kurdistan, and Anatolia."

During his short stay in Cairo the following supplementary instructions were communicated to General Gordon by Sir Evelyn Baring :—

" Lord Granville ' authorised and instructed you to perform such duties as the Egyptian Government may desire to intrust to you, and as may be communicated to you by Sir E. Baring.' I have now to indicate to you the views of the Egyptian Govern-ment on two of the points to which your special attention was directed by Lord Granville. These are (1) the measures which it may be advisable to take for the security of the Egyptian garrisons still holding positions in the Soudan, and for the safety of the European population in Khartoum. (2) The best mode of effecting the evacuation of the interior of the Soudan. These two points are intimately connected, and may con-veniently be considered together. It is believed that the num-ber of Europeans at Khartoum is very small, but it has been estimated by the local authorities that some 10,000 to 15,000 people will wish to move northwards from Khartoum only when the Egyptian garrison is withdrawn. These people are native

Christians, Egyptian employés, their wives and children, &c.
The Government of his Highness the Khedive is earnestly soli-
citous that no effort should be spared to insure the retreat both
of these people and of the Egyptian garrison without loss of life.
As regards the most opportune time and the best method for
effecting the retreat, whether of the garrisons or of the civil
populations, it is neither necessary nor desirable that you should
receive detailed instructions. A short time ago the local authorities pressed strongly on the Egyptian Government the necessity for giving orders for an immediate retreat. Orders were accordingly given to commence at once the withdrawal of the civil
population. No sooner, however, had these orders been issued
than a telegram was received from the Soudan, strongly urging that
the orders for commencing the retreat immediately should be delayed. Under these circumstances, and in view of the fact that
the position at Khartoum is now represented as being less
critical for the moment than it was a short time ago, it was
thought desirable to modify the orders for the immediate retreat
of the civil population, and to await your arrival. You will bear
in mind that the main end to be pursued is the evacuation of
the Soudan. This policy was adopted, after very full discus-
sion, by the Egyptian Government, on the advice of Her
Majesty's Government. It meets with the full approval of his
Highness the Khedive, and of the present Egyptian Ministry.
I understand also that you entirely concur in the desirability of
adopting this policy, and that you think it should on no account
be changed. You consider that it may take a few months to
carry it out with safety. You are further of opinion that 'the
restoration of the country should be made to the different petty
Sultans who existed at the time of Mohammed Ali's, conquest,
and whose families still exist ;' and that an endeavour should be
made to form a confederation of those Sultans. In this view
the Egyptian Government entirely concur. It will, of course,
be fully understood that the Egyptian troops are not to be kept
in the Soudan merely with a view to consolidating the power of
the new rulers of the country. But the Egyptian Government
has the fullest confidence in your judgment, your knowledge of
the country, and of your comprehension of the general line of
policy to be pursued. You are therefore given full discretionary

power to retain the troops for such reasonable period as you may think necessary, in order that the abandonment of the country may be accomplished with the least possible risk of life and property. A credit of £100,000 has been opened for you at the Finance Department, and further funds will be supplied to you on your requisition when this sum is exhausted. In undertaking the difficult task which now lies before you, you may feel assured that no effort will be wanting on the part of the Cairo authorities, whether English or Egyptians, to afford you all the co-operation and support in their power."

This paper Sir Evelyn read to General Gordon, and reported to Lord Granville that he expressed entire concurrence in the instructions it embodies. The only suggestion he made was in connection with the passage in which Sir Evelyn, speaking of the policy of abandoning the Soudan, had said, " I understand also that you entirely concur in the desirability of adopting this policy." General Gordon had desired Sir Evelyn to add the words, "and that you think it should on no account be changed." Those words were accordingly embodied in the document.

While Gordon and his companion were crossing the desert, there had occurred another of those stupendous massacres with which the history of the Soudan is so thickly studded. On February 4th General Baker's Egyptian force, marching from Trinkitat toward Tokar with intent to relieve the garrison of that beleaguered place, had been attacked by a detachment of Osman Digna's Arab levies, defeated almost without resistance, and with a loss of nearly two-thirds of its number, utterly annihilated as a military force. Under popular pressure, the British Government had formed the resolve of despatching to the Eastern Soudan an expeditionary force of British troops charged with the duty, if there should be yet time, of relieving the garrisons of Sinkat and Tokar; contingently, however, on General Gordon's reply to the question addressed to him, asking whether this measure met with his approval. As soon as—having emerged safely from the desert—he had recovered his communications, he replied, "not very enthusiastically," that he saw no particular objections; and the experiences of General Graham's little army do not come within the province of this little volume.

It was on the 11th February that General Gordon reached Berber, "in high spirits and very sanguine as to the success of his mission." He threw himself into his work with all his old energy. Before leaving Berber he confirmed

Hussein Bey Halifa in the governorship, strengthening his position by giving him a Council of Notables, and he sent forward orders to Khartoum removing Hussein Pasha from the Vice-Governor-Generalship, and appointing in his room Colonel de Coetlogen, who had been in military charge ever since the catastrophe which befell Hicks Pasha's army. In advance of General Gordon's arrival in the capital, the city was placarded with a proclamation sent forward by him, proclaiming the Mahdi Sultan of Kordofan, remitting one-half of the taxes, and permitting the trade in slaves to be carried on. The proclamation is said to have given universal satisfaction. The *Times* correspondent communicated a conversation with an intelligent Arab : " Gordon Pasha," said the Arab, "will be received as a friend of the Arabs and blacks. His coming means no more Turks, with their backsheesh and kourbash. But he should have come a year ago ; it is now too late." Gordon himself did not think it was too late, if we are to judge by the telegram he sent Sir Evelyn Baring from Berber :—

"Am leaving for Khartoum, and believe you need not give yourself any further anxiety about this part of the Soudan. The people, great and small, are heartily glad to be free from a union which has only caused them sorrow."

It was on the morning of Tuesday, February 18th, that General Gordon made his entry into Khartoum. In one of his letters home he describes how when entering Keren àrrayed in the splendid "gold coat" of a field marshal, and in the pomp beseeming the Governor-General of the Soudan, the humour of his fancy had suggested to him some resemblance in the eyes of the populace between him and "the Divine Figure from the North" who was just then a good deal in the mouths of men. A veritable "Divine Figure" he must have shone in the sight of the people of Khartoum as he came among them on this February morning. What a change for them from the *régime* of Bashi-Bashoukery, of the pashas, of the stick, the lash, the prison; from the grinding taxation and the denial of even a form of justice! No wonder that as he passed to the Palace from the Mudirieh, where he had been holding a levee to which the poorest Arab was admitted, the people pressed about him, kissing his hands and feet, and hailing him as "Sultan," "Father," and

"Saviour!" There is a whole-souled energy and an uncompromising thoroughness in everything that this man does. With the best will in the world to redress grievances, another man would have gone about the work in a methodical, un-galvanic fashion. But Gordon does not know the meaning of routine. There on the shelves were the Government ledgers, on whose pages were the long records of the outstanding debts that weighed down the over-taxed people. On the walls hung the kourbashes, whips, and bas-tinado rods, implements of tyranny and torture. Gordon wiped out the evidence of debts and destroyed the emblems of oppression in a fine impulse of characteristic ardour. A fire was made in front of the palace, and the books and bastinado rods thrown on this funeral pyre of Egyptian tyranny.

He had so but begun the day's work. From the council chamber he hurried to the hospital, thence to inspect the arsenal. Then he darted to the heart of the misery of the prison. In that loathsome den two hundred wretched beings were rotting in their chains. Young and old, condemned and untried, the proven innocent and the arrested on suspicion, he found all clotted together in one mass of common suffering. With wrathful disgust, Gordon set about the summary work of liberation. Before night fell the chains had fallen from off scores of the miserables, and the beneficent labour was being steadily pursued. Ere this busy day closed Gordon's energy had left him hardly anything to do inside of Khartoum. He had arranged that the Soudanese soldiers were to stay in their native land, and had appointed to the command of them a veteran negro officer, who had distinguished himself in Mexico under Bazaine. He had settled that the Egyptian soldiers were to be sent across the river to Am Durman, where was Hicks's camp before he started on his ill-fated march, and that they and their families were to be sent down the river in detachments, and so also were to go the European civilians who cared to leave.

And here, while he stands on the threshold of this latest and most arduous enterprise of all, this brief record will leave him. What has occurred since General Gordon arrived in Khartoum is yet clouded and misty. Shadows have fallen across the brightness of the early landscape, and his buoyant anticipations are

not finding realisation. It may be that this
task which he has undertaken shall prove
impossible for him to accomplish. But down
in the country whence he sprang there is a
homely proverb, "A stout heart to a stey
brae." No difficulties will abate his loyal
courage; no stress of adversity will daunt his
gallant heart. For him life has no ambition,
death no terror. He will do his duty.

THE END.

BRADBURY, AGNEW, & CO., PRINTERS, WHITEFRIARS.

Trieste

Trieste Publishing has a massive catalogue of classic book titles. Our aim is to provide readers with the highest quality reproductions of fiction and non-fiction literature that has stood the test of time. The many thousands of books in our collection have been sourced from libraries and private collections around the world.

The titles that Trieste Publishing has chosen to be part of the collection have been scanned to simulate the original. Our readers see the books the same way that their first readers did decades or a hundred or more years ago. Books from that period are often spoiled by imperfections that did not exist in the original. Imperfections could be in the form of blurred text, photographs, or missing pages. It is highly unlikely that this would occur with one of our books. Our extensive quality control ensures that the readers of Trieste Publishing's books will be delighted with their purchase. Our staff has thoroughly reviewed every page of all the books in the collection, repairing, or if necessary, rejecting titles that are not of the highest quality. This process ensures that the reader of one of Trieste Publishing's titles receives a volume that faithfully reproduces the original, and to the maximum degree possible, gives them the experience of owning the original work.

We pride ourselves on not only creating a pathway to an extensive reservoir of books of the finest quality, but also providing value to every one of our readers. Generally, Trieste books are purchased singly - on demand, however they may also be purchased in bulk. Readers interested in bulk purchases are invited to contact us directly to enquire about our tailored bulk rates. Email: customerservice@triestepublishing.com

You May Also Like

Hour by Hour; Or, The Christian's Daily Life

E. A. L.

ISBN: 9780649607242
Paperback: 172 pages
Dimensions: 6.14 x 0.37 x 9.21 inches
Language: eng

The Works of James Russell Lowell, Vol. VII. The Poetical Works of James Russell Lowell, in Four Volumes, Vol. I

James Russell Lowell

ISBN: 9780649640430
Paperback: 332 pages
Dimensions: 6.14 x 0.69 x 9.21 inches
Language: eng

You May Also Like

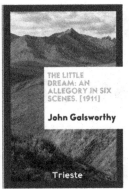

The Little Dream: An Allegory in Six Scenes. [1911]

John Galsworthy

ISBN: 9780649637270
Paperback: 50 pages
Dimensions: 6.14 x 0.10 x 9.21 inches
Language: eng

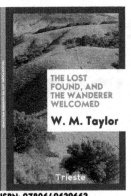

The Lost Found, and the Wanderer Welcomed

W. M. Taylor

ISBN: 9780649639663
Paperback: 188 pages
Dimensions: 6.14 x 0.40 x 9.21 inches
Language: eng

You May Also Like

ISBN: 9780649336067
Paperback: 84 pages
Dimensions: 6.14 x 0.17 x 9.21 inches
Language: eng

The Ancient Burial Mounds of Japan, pp. 511-522

Romyn Hitchcock

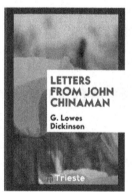

ISBN: 9780649333684
Paperback: 82 pages
Dimensions: 6.14 x 0.17 x 9.21 inches
Language: eng

Letters from John Chinaman

G. Lowes Dickinson

You May Also Like

Wah Sing, Our Little Chinese Cousin

Helen L. Campbell

ISBN: 9780649329861
Paperback: 78 pages
Dimensions: 6.14 x 0.16 x 9.21 inches
Language: eng

Water-colors: Four Chinese Tone Poems

John Alden Carpenter

ISBN: 9780649225736
Paperback: 36 pages
Dimensions: 6.14 x 0.08 x 9.21 inches
Language: eng

Find more of our titles on our website. We have a selection of thousands of titles that will interest you. Please visit

www.triestepublishing.com

Lightning Source UK Ltd.
Milton Keynes UK
UKOW01f1323231017
311488UK00017B/3803/P